The Sun King

Allison Lee Palmer

Open Books

Author's Note

The primary events of this story are real, and unfold over an eighteenth-month time span (September 2013—March 2015) that includes an imaginary backstory. The people and places all exist, but sometimes in an embellished context and with a different description to protect the privacy of everyone involved.

This book is dedicated
to the memory of
John Robert "Jack" Ruder (1995–2017).
I wish he stuck around a little bit longer.

Contents

Here in Oklahoma

Here in Oklahoma, the earth does not reach up to meet the sky but the ground lies flat and motionless while the heavens rush down to collapse on top of it. I am never prepared for the wind, which does not caress the earth gently, but thrusts itself across the plain, smoothing out any potential hills on the earth's surface. A few trees, bent by the weight of the atmosphere leaning on their branches, hunker down as if waiting for the next ice storm. Standing on my porch one night, I squint my eyes toward their tortured silhouettes and wonder if I, too, will suffer the same fate one day if I do not attempt to resist gravity.

Before I moved to Oklahoma, I bought an atlas. I remember twirling the circular mileage wheel in the back of the book to see how far I was from Rome, then from Boston. The mileage moved from four digits to three when I matched the wheel to St. Louis, then to Dallas. It was too far to fathom.

It should be known, however, that as a child I woke up startled one hot summer evening, sweating and crying, feeling a sharp longing for Oklahoma, a place I had never been to. What made this strange melancholy even more peculiar was at that time I knew nothing about Oklahoma except it was one of the odd-shaped wooden pieces in my puzzle of the United States. I remember assembling my puzzle over and over again, moving each state deftly into place, reaffirming the geography of the United States with my tiny fingers.

I always began with the east coast, where I lived, and after I smoothed out my bedspread and lined all the pieces up in alphabetical order, I worked methodically to fit them together by moving from east to north, west to the south, before venturing into the middle of the country. I wedged the puzzle piece of Oklahoma into place last because it had this awkward shape with a narrow stem of wood sticking out on one side that I had to wiggle into a tight spot above Texas and next to New Mexico. After appreciating how Oklahoma anchored all the other states securely into place, I turned the puzzle upside-down and watched the United States tumble onto the floor.

Nowadays, sometimes I tumble onto the floor, like a rag doll, and I wait patiently for someone to pick up my limp body and place me carefully onto the couch somewhere. I try to think of how I look lying crumpled on the floor—maybe I look very dramatic. Gray spots cloud my eyes, causing me to reach out desperately to clutch whoever is standing near me while politely explaining that I will be falling down in a moment, and would you please catch me?

I am usually caught before I slump to the ground, and I am gently guided downward slowly with my head carefully cushioned by a jacket, a sweater, even a book. At times friends have been confronted with this task, but it is most often a perfect stranger to whom I whisper the question: "Will you catch me?" The person turns to me, usually perplexed, then reaches out to me, reaches out to catch my fall. I grab the unfamiliar arm for support, like an old friend, while the blood drains from my face.

When I regain consciousness, I do not open my eyes at first, but I take a moment to enjoy the strange situation I am in, because maybe I am lying flat out in the middle of a shop floor, a sidewalk, or even in a street. I lie there pretending to be unconscious, contemplating what type of person will be there, hunched over me, curious and protective, what face will be looking down at me when I open my eyes, what eyes will stare earnestly into mine.

Sometimes a hand will instinctively caress my flushed cheeks with an unreserved tenderness that brings tears to my eyes. I take my unplanned fall as a leisurely respite, savoring the haziness of my surroundings until this stranger clasps my hands and waist, encouraging me to stand up. Once I say that I am fine now and I begin to move away, the person always lingers a moment longer to make certain that I am speaking the truth. As I turn away, I know this person's eyes will follow my image until I disappear into the distance, assessing how I move through space to see if I will stumble and fall again.

Here in Oklahoma the sky pushes down on me like I am the earth, forcing me to spend many warm evenings lying on the floor of my house, breathless. On those nights the moon casts shadows that dance across my porch, and on some nights I can hear a wolf (or perhaps a dog) howl in the distance.

During these long evenings I have started to rethink my memories, organizing them into groups, altering certain aspects of them, cleaning others out of my brain and replacing them with new memories. It is a huge, mental spring cleaning that I must do before I can figure out what I will eventually tell my son about me, what I will tell him about himself, and what I will tell other people about the two of us. Therefore, I must say right from the beginning that most of this story is true, but not all of it.

CHAPTER ONE

The Sun King

My son was born the Sun King, the Sagittarius baby with his arms flung out from his sides riding on the back of a horse through a field of sunflowers, naked except for the row of small yellow daisies woven through his long, golden hair and the jaunty feather rising above his head. In my mind's eye I see him holding in his left hand a large red banner that unfurls around his little body while above him the sun shines rays of yellow light upon his little head. He is the boy-wonder, who, now an eighteen-year old man-child poised on the threshold of legal adulthood, rages in anger at his plight.

"Why did they take my tie?" he questions me, with his blue eyes blazing black.

This time there is no escape through the locked doors behind which he paces back and forth.

My son Jack now stands 6 feet 2 inches tall in front of me, and I can tell he has lost weight by the way his clothing hangs loosely from his thin frame. He is wearing a khaki suit with a button-down oxford shirt, no tie, no belt, and thick woolen socks on his feet. His shoulders are broad and strong from years of competitive swimming, and his jacket fits neatly across his chest but sways down his torso while his long arms jut out too soon from the sleeves. His shaggy dark blond hair is cut short on the sides and left long on the top, which allows thick chunks of hair to wave wildly across his face. He has worn the same outfit for five days now, but his rumpled clothing still smells clean thanks to a daily schedule of lying in bed or pacing around the hospital lounge all day long.

I had just been let into the foyer of Rose Hill Behavioral Health Hospital at 6 p.m. sharp to visit Jack for one hour. I am staying in a dingy hotel not too far from the hospital but I still got lost finding the correct entrance because the mental health buildings are set back from the street, hidden behind a row of trees lining this pretty Ohio road. Coming from Oklahoma, I am not used to the thick, lush, September vegetation that obscures my view.

I also have a tiny rental car, and as I was driving across town in my exhausted state, I had to remind myself over and over again to navigate the car slowly and carefully because I couldn't remember if I had purchased the extra car insurance when I picked the vehicle up at the airport, and I knew that if I wrecked the car Jack would be waiting for me, confused and cut off from the world, not knowing why I didn't show up.

Jack was indeed waiting for me in the visitor's room, and when I arrived he swooped down and lifted me off my feet in a big bear hug; he was clearly glad to see me, especially since I was the person who was going to spring him free from this undignified entrapment. So I wrapped my arms around my tall son, inhaled deeply to breathe in his smell that I had known since he was born, and we turned to sit next to each other at one of the round tables. He immediately forgot about his tie and flung himself on the floor, inviting me to abandon my chair for a spot on the carpet next to him. Now we were both on the floor, sitting with our legs crisscrossed applesauce, facing each other.

"Meditation is very important, you know," he said to me while shifting to the lotus pose, but he was panting and giggling, barely able to keep still. I could see his hands were shaking while his forehead shined with a thin layer of sweat. Suddenly another thought occurred to him and his smile disappeared.

"Why is it that every time I share my ideas,

I end up in the hospital?" he asked, becoming visibly upset by this revelation. I could tell that he was thinking of how his *magnum opus* had been derailed once again by all the doctors who should have known better, and his plans to save the world were temporarily foiled.

Just as abruptly as he sat down, Jack now jumped up from the floor and marched into the nurses' office where two women looked up from a stack of files they were sorting and stared at him in dismay. Oblivious to their discomfort at this security breach, Jack picked up a few sheets of paper from the recycling bin, grabbed a pencil off the table and returned to the visitor's room, where he plopped back down in the chair at the round table.

As I got up from the floor, Jack began to draw a big circle, and with several long strokes of the pencil he divided it into pie-shaped wedges that demonstrated the sleep pattern of Leonardo da Vinci, who, he claimed, practiced a polyphasic sleep that included a 20-minute nap every six hours, four times in every 24-hour cycle, never sleeping a full night. In this way, Jack argued, Leonardo da Vinci had enough time to generate all the ideas needed to change the world.

And this was what Jack planned to do—never sleep so that he could spend all twenty-four hours of each day changing the world. But then things kept getting in the way and nobody believed this would be possible; instead doctors spoke of gluta-mate overstimulation. Glutamate, not dopamine, is the major nerve-transmitter culprit in psy-chosis, and glutamic acid, an amino acid, is also implicated in seizures, which is why anti-seizure medicine is sometimes used in a mood disorder. This precise medicine was the divalproex sodium that Jack had been spitting out into the drawer of his desk for the past three months.

Because I found his pills there, some of which were brand new while others were partially dis-solved in dried saliva, I spent the entire summer researching and assembling an impressive array of supplements and vitamins for an adjunctive treatment plan that I thought would accomplish the same goal. I included a low-dose aspirin to help interrupt the neurotoxic cascades by reduc-ing inflammation, vitamin C to protect the body from excess vanadium, vitamin D (D is for Depression), omega 3 for brain health, NAC in the morning, and 5-HTP in the evening. I also learned that one could avoid gluten and caseins in food because chronic inflammation can perhaps cause neural changes such as dendritic remodel-ing and glial and neuro-cell loss together with an over-activity of the hypothalamic-pituitary-ad-renal axis.

The thing is, I read all of this on the internet but I didn't really know what any of it meant because I was a museum educator, yet I had a sick child who was trying to be a college student and I wanted specific and detailed information so he could be cured. And, since he wouldn't take his medicine, doctors refused to talk to him or me, so I tried my best to learn some pharmacology to make the healing happen with herbal remedies available at the local health food store.

Aside from medicine, there was one other thing I also learned to be of utmost importance—more crucial than a nutritional program—is the need for sleep. A lack of sleep must always be dealt with swiftly and aggressively, but this was precisely what did not happen when my son went to college.

Instead, on the third weekend of Jack's first semester, flush with cash from his summer job and his first work-study paycheck, he planned the party of the century in his dorm room with enough alcohol and drugs to fuel every student on his version of the Titanic. This was in addition to the necessary purchases of an embossed silver cigarette case needed to cut a sharp figure at the party, and a second phone because one was not enough to handle the huge number of text messages and emails he was receiving from all his new friends. Nine hundred dollars spent in 45 minutes.

The party was a hit, with music blasting and warm bodies swaying against each other in the crowded room. Plastic cups sloshed brown liquid while conversations weaved through the thumping drumbeats and loud shouts of a newly drunken freshman class. As the evening wore on into the early morning, students gradually drifted back to their rooms and tumbled into their beds to sleep the heavy, unhurried sleep that is the gift of youth.

Unbeknownst to all of them, however, was the fact that World War III was brewing outside, and Jack did not want the party to end because he reasoned it would be the last party on earth. Instead, he hunkered down by a shade tree outside his dormitory, now all alone and still wide awake, to continue his own version of the festivities on the other side of reality.

It was at 6:18 a.m. when my phone beeped, and since I was slightly awake, I glanced at the screen to find a text message from Jack that read:

"I'll meet you on the other side."

Suddenly I was completely awake and jumping out of bed with my fingers shaking across the numbers of my phone trying to call him. My frantic phone calls remained unanswered, however, and so, as I kept repeating to myself, "Do not panic, do not panic, do not panic, do not panic," I turned on my computer, typed in the college's website, found the phone number for campus security, which I called, and I asked the man on the other end of the telephone to find Jack and please not let him leave his sight until I could get there.

Right then I wanted to be a spider spinning a thread—the thread of life—and I wanted to cast this thread toward Jack so it would encircle him and protect him. But since I am not a spider, I drove to the airport and got on a plane that took off at exactly 9 a.m. and carried me through the clear, blue sky across four states and over 930 miles so that I could extend the golden thread of life from me to my first-born child and reveal to him the shining path of consciousness bound to matter that ties us to this carnal world.

———————

Jack had been rescued by strangers, by people who had led him gently by the arm to an ambulance and to the hospital emergency room, from where he was transferred to a wing that was locked to the outside world. While all of this was happening, I sat in a metal tube hurtling through the sky, trying desperately to keep my brain tamped down as if I were breathing underwater, away from the light and sounds of thoughts too horrifying to entertain.

Jack was now staring straight at me. "Are you not even listening?" he asked, bringing my thoughts back to the present. After explaining Leonardo's sleep pattern, he shifted in his chair and gazed at me with an imperious stare; suddenly he realized why I was there, and he made it clear to me that he did not want my revelations, my golden thread.

What did I know about anything?

According to him, I refused to delve into my subconscious mind and therefore I was unable to achieve a deeper understanding of the meaning of life. I was tied to the materiality of my existence, while his solipsistic detachment from the physical world allowed him to negate all that surrounded him to achieve an abstract, enlightened state of consciousness. He gleefully anticipated the day when we could transcend our human condition with a new technology that would allow us to download the entire content of our brains into a computer and live a disembodied existence for eternity.

"Singularity is near!" he proclaimed from the middle of the visitor's room, the self-designated mental hospital messiah. "If we can make it to 2045, we'll be able to attain immortality."

It was the Maya calendar, adjusted slightly. It was the Rapture for the technophile; it was *technologia amans*. It was where you went when humanity became too boring.

———

Three days later, the doctor considered Jack well enough to leave the hospital. We had a brief meeting with several staff members, and my son, now hoping to become a psychiatrist when he finished college, quizzed the doctor about the medical profession. Then we signed the release papers and insurance forms and Jack's possessions were returned to him in a large plastic bag that held a rusty wrench and a long flathead screwdriver, two large metal bolts, the beautiful and expensive silver cigarette case, two phones, and a camera with several rolls of film shot during the party of the century. Jack carefully reviewed his belongings and read the inventory list, checking off each item before signing the bottom of the form. I made a mental note to have the rolls of film developed the next morning.

The nurse handed him a customer satisfaction survey to fill out and he laughed while decorating the form with random scribbles and smiley faces before handing both forms back to the nurse with a big grin on his face. In the three days that Jack had been hospitalized, he had gone from heavily medicated and sleepy to awake and angry to utterly charming, each day with more medicine coursing through his veins.

Before we left the hospital, Jack lumbered over to the petite nurse, swooped down to her level and gave her a big farewell hug. I saw a flash a fear in her eyes that quickly dissolved into relief as she laughed haltingly and cautiously hugged him back. Then Jack stormed out the now unlocked door, stopped to breathe the fresh air, and fell to the ground to kiss the grass. I clutched his two-week supply of aripiprazole while trying to dismiss the fearful look of the farewell nurse from my mind.

Aripiprazole is the drug advertised in every fashion magazine, the tiny blue pill that lets you sleep at night and think clearly during the day. Only the medicine won't work, I soon discovered, because Jack had already decided not to take it.

As we walked slowly toward the rental car, Jack turned to look at me with a conspiratorial smile on his face; I was his accomplice. He continued to look at me, now with a leering expression, as I opened the car door and threw his plastic bag and medicine bottle in the back seat.

I pulled out of the parking lot while he turned the radio to an '80s music station and cranked up the volume until I felt the music thumping in my chest. He nodded his head wildly to the beat while I steered the car back to campus and dropped him off at his dorm.

Then I sat in the car, not sure of what to do next while I watched him disappear through the entrance. This was when I began to realize that Jack and I were playing a game of chess, only it was his game, with a new set of rules where he was the king and I was his pawn.

CHAPTER TWO

The Moon Children

I see the moon and the moon sees me
shining through the leaves of the old oak tree.
Oh, let the light that shines on me
shine on the one I love.

(Irish author, date unknown)

One year ago on a mid-September Sunday in the late afternoon I was playing the violin when Jack, a high school senior, was first arrested. I had begun a habit of hiding the car keys and my money, but it was a warm fall day and Jack was studying in his room while I practiced for my upcoming concert, and so I left my car keys on the kitchen counter. After a while I thought I heard the keys clink together, then the back door open and close, but for reasons that remain unknown to me even today, I kept playing. Jack left the house to the strains of Fauré's *Berceuse*, right at the part where I play the soft harmonics.

Why hadn't I stopped him? I knew his behavior had been somewhat odd recently, but sometimes my life unfolds in a series of non-decisions and non-actions, and this was one of those moments.

I did become worried, however, so I put away my violin and called Jack's cell phone over and over again. Finally his phone was answered, not by Jack, but by a police officer. The officer told me he had arrested my son for driving under the influence of drugs and alcohol, a DUI, and I thanked him profusely because that meant Jack was alive. People don't get arrested when they are dead, I reasoned, so this was good news indeed for a Sunday afternoon.

After I hung up the phone, however, I thought of how this story was suddenly starting to make sense, and not in a good way. My legs gave way to the carpet below, where I buried my face to muffle my cries.

While I was trying to contain myself, my very polite son was across town, staggering down the side of the road alongside a police officer, making small talk and apologizing for the trouble with the car, which was now up on the sidewalk with the front two tires shredded by stop sticks. The police officer handcuffed Jack and took him to the juvenile detention center while the car, which was my car, was towed to the police impound lot.

As for me, I got up off the floor, found the keys to my son's old Saab that hadn't been running lately, and I worked to get it started by holding the gear in neutral with my foot on the brake while turning the ignition switch until the engine came to life, and then I drove to the juvenile center.

Upon my arrival, Jack's calm demeanor turned to panic and then to anger as he began to consider various ways out of his predicament. He locked himself in the bathroom and punched the wall repeatedly until his hand broke, all the while I pleaded with the two workers, both of whom appeared to be barely over eighteen years of age, to unlock the bathroom door so I could check on him.

One of the workers, a young man with a round face, sat in his chair unconvinced this was a good idea, but to appease me he slowly sorted through a series of keys hanging on the wall behind him pretending he didn't know which one led to the bathroom, while the young woman sat frozen at her desk with a dazed look in her eyes, filling out forms with a ballpoint pen and shuffling through a set of folders like none of this was happening.

They did manage to call the police officer, however, who had left the building only a few moments earlier, and when the officer returned, the key magically appeared and Jack was pulled, bleeding, out of the bathroom and dragged into the office where he was put into a chair and handcuffed to one of the wooden chair slats. I sat down across from him and looked into his eyes, but all I saw was a blank, black, unfocused gaze, as if his mind had gone out into the abyss.

Jack then refocused on his present situation and proceeded to apologize for how he had damaged my car—the car that ran over the stop sticks that shredded the tires that jumped the curb that landed on the sidewalk that was impounded and towed away before I arrived. But I didn't care about that because I can buy a new car, I told him, but I can't buy a new son. So Jack was put back in the police car and I got into the Saab, managed to start the engine again, and I followed the policeman to the Children's Recover Center.

By now, several hours had passed, the sun had gone down, and the moon shone brightly in the sky. I continued to follow the police officer as he drove back into town, down Main Street, and when he got to Porter Avenue he turned right into the sprawling complex of buildings that was once the location of the state mental institution but is now the site of an assortment of old and new buildings used for a variety of state and county health services.

At first glance, the complex could easily have been mistaken for a college campus, except for the fact that two of the larger, old four-story brick buildings were completely abandoned, yet they still stood there solemnly displaying tall, wide porches with columns straining to support their roofs and white paint peeling off the wood trim. Crumbled concrete steps led down from the broad, empty porches and linked into sidewalks that at one time led people scurrying from one building to another. At one end of the complex was a tall, Neo-Gothic Catholic church, the last vestige of the adjoining nun's convent that was closed in the 1970s. Wooden boards covered the stained-glass windows that had been smashed to bits long ago.

Since that time, newer buildings had been constructed piecemeal across the complex, with sidewalks that made straight lines from buildings to their adjoining parking lots. These buildings had no names, just numbered signs clearly meant for visitors who already knew where they were going. Most of these buildings were closed for the night by now, and their parking lots were empty.

I continued to follow the police car as it drove past these buildings toward a dimly lit concrete structure at the end of the complex. This building had yellow light filtering out from dirty windows and two cars were parked in its lot. I turned into the parking lot and pulled into a space next to the police car. From there we all walked together, an odd trio, with the policeman in front but keeping a sharp eye on Jack, and me with my arm snaked around my son's elbow that was held behind his back by the handcuffs that linked his wrists together.

The police officer pressed the inconspicuous buzzer located to the side of the door, announced his name, and the door clicked open. We walked into this yellow-glowing building that I had driven past for many years on my way to the grocery store and the dog park, but I had never once wondered what it was until now. Now I had, by reason of my son's emerging lunacy, permission to enter this building for the first time in my life.

That is when I realized this is the building where the moonchildren live, closed behind thick walls in a world unknown to the rest of us. I never saw their eyes peering out the small, dirty windows as I drove by, so I didn't know. This is where the young prophets receive their holy visions while their fathers drive to work and their mothers shop at Walmart. This is where the children of the night learn to navigate a daytime world that is nothing but a great disappointment to their finely tuned hopes and desires. And this is where these children either give in to their despair and howl at the moon, or get down on their hands and knees and crawl out of the murky water like a lobster in its shell to follow the luminous path carved out of the earth's surface by the ones who love them:

God looked down on me from above
And He gave you to me for me to love,
Please let the light that shines on me
Shine on the one I love.

Later that same night, Jack, a nurse, and I sat around a table lit by a long fluorescent bulb and made a plan. The plan involved filling out an enormous amount of paperwork under the seizure-inducing glare of the harsh light until midnight, while all three of us tried to make sense of what was going on. My eyes clung to the eyes of the nurse as if I were on a life raft and she my savior, but although I tried my best to read a message in her gaze that would explain what was happening, she looked back at me blandly, in the middle of her typical work day, and handed me another form to sign. She had seen this before and certainly knew things that I didn't know, but she was the keeper of information and I was on the outside.

After decisions were made and forms were signed, Jack and I had to part ways, so I slipped out the door that the nurse carefully held open a few inches for me, while my son was led further inside the building, down a hall in the opposite direction.

It was almost 1 a.m. by the time I arrived

home, and I sat on my living room floor thinking through the day's events. I couldn't get rid of the image burned in my brain of the blank stare I saw in Jack's eyes that afternoon, a look I hoped never to see again. Then I went to bed feeling an odd sense of comfort knowing exactly where Jack was. There would be no climbing out his bedroom window that night.

When Jack woke up the next morning, he couldn't remember the events of the previous night but he saw that he was lying on a thin mattress in a twin bed located in a smallish room across from another twin bed where a blond-haired boy who looked about fifteen years old was still sleeping. The room had one chunky desk and an old wooden chair, but it was otherwise empty. It looked like a run-down dorm room, but where? He felt sick, but the room was too dingy and quiet to be in a hospital, so maybe it was a jail cell, except that jail cells don't have chunky wooden furniture, do they?

He got up out of bed, and although he felt woozy, he walked over to the desk and leaned across it to peer out a dirty corner window, where, by looking sharply left, he could see part of the eastside Walmart across the intersection of Porter and Main Street. It was then that he knew where he was—inside the one-story concrete building set back from the street behind a parking lot that was next to the alternative high school. He had driven past this building so many times but he didn't know what it was, and now he had miraculously woken up inside one of its rooms.

When I got out of bed that same morning after not sleeping at all, I didn't remember to call the high school and tell them Jack was sick, so I went to work and shuffled through the day until it was time to go home. At home, I changed into jeans and a T-shirt while my answering machine beeped to tell me that my son had an unexplained absence from school that day. The first evening visitation at the Children's Recovery Center was at 6 p.m., so I drove straight there without eating and arrived in the visiting area stripped of my possessions except for my plastic identification card and the take-out sushi that I knew would be Jack's meal request.

A sign in the foyer read: "No guns, no knifes, no drugs," but Jesus, who brings these, I wondered loud enough to elicit a response from the security guard, "You'd be surprised," he said, slowly shaking his head.

I looked over at him. "Jesus," was all I could think of to say.

Through the metal detector, I passed into the dining area where my son was hunched over a table, staring glumly at nothing in particular. At the next table sat a mother and father flanking their daughter, who was slumped down in a pose identical to that of Jack. The rest of the room was filled with similar groupings of visitors paired with a teenager who was slumped down and staring at their tables, and nobody looked up to acknowledge anyone else, nobody made eye contact, nobody nodded hello. Nobody working there said: "Welcome!" or, "It's good to see you!" It clearly wasn't that kind of place.

I slipped quietly into a chair across from Jack and slid the sushi over to him. He straightened up a bit and reached for the food, snapping open the plastic container and slipping the paper off the chopsticks.

"I skipped dinner tonight," he said between bites.

"What time was dinner?" I asked, looking at my watch that now said 6:15 p.m.

"I don't know," he responded. After that we barely spoke. Neither of us knew what was going to unfold, but I certainly thought this was the bottom, which is sometimes called "rock bottom." In my mind, rock bottom was sort-of like when you are diving underwater and you hit your head on some rocks, but you still manage to do a flip turn even though you are bleeding, and you start to come back up in order to breath oxygen once again. Jack was a strong swimmer, I thought to myself, so he could do this. I felt certain there was a cure for whatever it was that ailed him; I knew there had to be.

Indeed, we quickly found out the diagnosis was major depression, and the cure was Prozac, according to the doctors. I had heard about Prozac, it was so over-prescribed across the nation that somebody even made a movie about it.

Therefore, at first we said no to Prozac, but then we decided yes to Prozac, 20 mgs, once a day. Jack didn't want this to be the answer, but I did, desperately. One pill, once a day, makes you all better! In fact, my son did seem to get better over the next few days, and so he was released ten days later with a bottle of pink pills.

During the summer before all this happened, Jack had been thinking about his college applications, or maybe I was the one thinking about his college applications, it's hard to separate these things out. At any rate, we had planned to visit a few schools throughout the fall, and it just so happened that the day after he was released from the recovery center was the day we were scheduled to fly to his first college interview. Therefore, after he was released from the center, I threaded his laces back into his tennis shoes, washed his clothes and re-packed his bags for the flight to Seattle.

The next morning we boarded a plane hoping

to put the entire health scare behind us now that we had a diagnosis and a cure. But…college interviews straight out of a crisis center, on Prozac? In hindsight, I must say I do not recommend this at all.

———

September became October, and fall became winter. During this time Jack's eyes shone with a passion I had never seen before, a passion that inspired him to think up a Dream Machine and build a spaceship. The spaceship was the setting for a short film called *The Cosmos* he made in his senior-year media class that won him entry into a summer arts camp.

Originally a small project, the spaceship soon began to consume all of Jack's time and he started skipping his other classes to work on it, spending hours taping large sections of cardboard together with shiny silver duct tape to create several rooms, and then smoothing aluminum foil up and down each section to cover every surface so the walls looked like they were made of shimmering metal.

The spaceship filled the studio room next to the editing lab at the high school, and its tall walls were then duct taped to the carpet for added stability while sections of the cardboard were cut out to make room for computer dashboards and air conditioning units painted black to resemble the mechanics of a flight deck.

During this time, I would on some days show up unexpectedly to see if Jack was in the editing lab when he was supposed to be elsewhere, and I would drag him to the class he was skipping, much to the dismay of the other media students, who wanted to help with the spaceship instead of doing their own schoolwork.

The spaceship project received the full support of the media instructors as well as a large number of student volunteers, all of whom lined up to crawl through the interior rooms and perform the role of the astronaut, lost in space and resigned to death while sitting next to the nonfunctional control panels with tears rolling down his or her face. It was all very dramatic.

In retrospect, I would argue that not only should the purchase of copious amounts of aluminum foil and cardboard be a warning sign at least mentioned in the Diagnostic and Statistical Manual of Mental Disorders, but the constant need for high drama should also be noted in the DSM, because all together they can only lead to the building of this spaceship that matches the criteria for Bipolar Disorder I. But I didn't know that until later.

Jack's spaceship prevented him from completing his chemistry assignments and his plans for a Dream Machine did not allow him time for his history homework. Instead, the media center continued to draw him in. It became his safe place, his domain, where he could be a master engineer consumed with the creation of something important, all the while outside the room everything else in his life was falling apart.

Then, in early December, Jack abruptly disassembled the spaceship, leaving large holes in the media room carpet, and brought the cardboard boxes home from school for future reassembly in his bedroom as a sensory deprivation chamber. The space odyssey film he had made that fall was finished, but the film was never screened and the project was never discussed again. The Dream Machine, however, continued to exert a pull on Jack's imagination in many ways over the next year.

CHAPTER THREE

The Ace of Swords (reversed)

When the ball starts rolling down the hill, how do you stop it? You don't. Instead, you keep working on your college applications as if everything is A-OK. That is exactly what Jack did—he wrote his college essays on neuroscience and photography, submitted his high school transcripts and test scores, and asked for letters of recommendation while I completed the financial aid forms.

He finished up the fall semester of his senior year of high school by taking apart his spaceship, barely passing his classes, and then we bought Christmas gifts and drove across the country to attend a family holiday seven states away. All the while I wondered what was happening to Jack. Despite my nagging sense of unease, we decided to stop for another college interview along the way, on the Friday of finals week, which was the last day the school was open before the holidays.

At this small college in Ohio, the students had all gone home and the campus was quiet and beautiful, with a thin covering of snow on the ground. We had brought our dog along with us on the road trip, so during Jack's interview I walked the dog in slow circles around the admissions building. While I pondered what sort of conversation was taking place behind the door of the interview room, my dog preoccupied himself with digging in the damp grass.

Maybe this wasn't the right time to look at colleges, I thought, but what did I know? Teenagers are an odd bunch anyway, not knowing who they are, not knowing what they want. After the interview, we drove on to my parent's home in Boston for the holidays, with Jack chattering away enthusiastically the entire trip.

We arrived three days before Christmas to a house filled with activity. My mother had planned several parties for our visit, so although we were exhausted, there was a lot to be done—cleaning the house, planning menus, and shopping for groceries. My sister, who just moved from Boston to Seattle last year, was spending Christmas with her in-laws, much to my mother's dismay, so my son and I started down the errand list as a team of two while my father made lists and my mother decorated the tree.

My sister and I were never particularly close when we were growing up. She was eight years older than me, so I was still in elementary school when she was in high school and she was in college when I was in middle school. During most of my youth I felt like an only child wandering around my parent's huge, old, quiet house filled with books and musical instruments. We grew close the year I returned from Rome, however, when I moved in with my sister while I finished college. That was the year Jack was born.

So this Christmas my mother made up my old bedroom for me. A tall, creaky antique bed had replaced my childhood bed and the room now had a television set, which was forbidden while I was growing up there. An extra bookshelf was squeezed next to my old dresser that held my father's textbooks from when he was in college. Jack was staying in my sister's old room down the hall that had been repainted white and repurposed as a study for my father, but with a twin bed in the corner.

Christmas Eve arrived together with all the guests for my mother's first dinner party of the season. Although the house was full of people, Jack spent most of the evening in his bedroom alone while our dog barked and cowered among the guests until I took him upstairs to contain him in my bedroom. All evening he frantically scratched at the door, clearly frightened of being alone. So my evening was spent running upstairs and downstairs, trying to cajole Jack to come downstairs while trying to keep the dog upstairs, all the while explaining to the guests that my son was not feeling well.

After an exhausting night filled with very little sleep, I woke before anyone else on Christmas morning and went downstairs to wash the remaining party dishes when I noticed an entire gallon bottle of rum nearly empty. I had carried the bottle to the kitchen last night and I knew it was full just before I went upstairs to bed at 2 a.m. A cold chill ran down my spine. I went upstairs to look in Jack's bedroom, where I hoped he might be asleep, but instead I found him wide awake, stripping the sheets off his bed and throwing them in the corner of the room.

"Please tell Grandmother I feel ill," he said in a haughty voice with a slight English accent. I stood there, rooted to the ground, not knowing what to say.

"Never mind, I'll tell her myself," he said, brushing past me. I heard him go down the hall, and then I could hear his voice talking to my mother, so I grabbed the vomit-filled sheets and ran down the back stairway to the laundry room. I rinsed the sheets in the sink and put them in the washer before walking back into the kitchen, where I saw my mother standing there, ashen. Jack was talking excitedly, but his tone of voice had changed, his vocabulary was different, he was using new types of phrases; it was like his entire perspective had shifted, maybe only slightly, or maybe not…. What was happening?

I asked him what happened to the rum. "Oh, I drank that," he answered casually, as if I had asked him about a glass of milk.

"Why?" I stammered as I tried to process my thoughts on the vast amount of alcohol that had disappeared.

"I need to drink enough to turn my brain off," Jack explained. Furthermore, he said he had planned to replace the missing liquor with water for the unsuspecting guests that were arriving to dinner that evening, but he decided he couldn't do that because our drinking water was poisoned.

I stared at him, dumbfounded, wondering how our drinking water was poisoned. Our drinking water had shown traces of chromium, I thought, just small amounts that were naturally occurring, so maybe this is what he was thinking…that we should be drinking bottled water? I asked him that, and he just stared at me.

Then, I thought back to a few days ago, on the evening we arrived. That evening, the hot water heater had broken and my father had a difficult time finding a repairman who could come the next morning since it was the holiday weekend. After many phone calls, he reached a man who agreed to stop by after lunch. Jack had seemed unusually anxious about this, not only because the hot water heater had broken on the day we arrived, but that the repairman couldn't come immediately.

Jack went on to clarify that these events were not a mere coincidence, but someone was purposefully trying to keep our water cold, since cold water is a more effective conduit for poison than hot water. I considered this explanation, and reasoned with myself that if someone were to actually believe that our drinking water was not potable, it would not be much of a leap to think that drinking a gallon of rum would perhaps be a safer and healthier alternative to tap water, sort-of like in the days of cholera on those tropical islands you read about.

Jack assumed my silence meant I was coming around to agreeing with his argument. "Don't worry, Mom. All teenagers are like this," he assured me. "You just don't understand."

I was beginning to understand one thing in all of this, which was that the holiday was not working out as planned. And so on this Christmas Day, after we awkwardly unwrapped our gifts and before the next set of guests arrived, I packed our bags, put the dog in the back seat of the car, and drove with Jack the entire way back to Oklahoma.

It was gray and moist outside when we left just short of noon, and I planned to drive over half way before stopping for the night, but since I had stayed up late last night by the evening I was too exhausted to drive any further. Not only had Jack lost his license with his September DUI, but he was also clearly in no shape to help me drive the twenty-two hours home anyway, so I pulled over at a nearly empty hotel where we checked in before crossing the street to see if there was anything to eat at the gas station, the only place open in town.

I bought two bananas, two sandwiches, some beef jerky for the dog, and an over-the-counter sleep aid for Jack, who had been wide awake the entire drive, talking and talking all the way, preparing his speech as high school class valedictorian. In his speech, he told me, he would focus on the idea that in the future, the person most qualified to save the world would be the scientist-artist, but the details of his reasoning were to be hashed out later.

Back in the hotel room, I made Jack take four times the normal dose of the sleep medication and promise me he wouldn't leave the room while I slept. By 11 p.m. the hotel and the town were completely dark, completely quiet, but Jack still couldn't sleep. I slept fitfully until 2 a.m., all while Jack sat bolt upright in his bed, staring around the room in an increasingly alarming state of panic. I knew he wouldn't be able to sit in the hotel room all night, so we got up, checked out of the hotel at 2:30 a.m., got back in the car, and I continued driving.

Somewhere in Missouri, I took a one-hour pre-dawn nap by the side of the road while I made Jack promise to stay in the back seat with the dog, and by the middle of the afternoon we made it across the border of Oklahoma, where I began to shift my thoughts to what we would do once we got home.

I felt like I was playing a game of chess and I had to figure out where to go, what my next move should be, but I was so tired I couldn't even think straight. It did briefly occur to me that I could change our destiny; I could veer off-plot. We could throw our cell phones out the window and continue driving out west like Butch Cassidy and the Sundance Kid. I was just so tired, though, and I yearned for my own bed.

So, instead we arrived back in our hometown by dinnertime, and although we were within arm's reach of our house, I knew that I had to drive straight to wherever one goes to get assessed for mental health issues because if we diverged from our self-appointed task even the slightest bit, all bets would be off—do not pass go, do not collect $200.

I was so achingly tired by now that I kept thumping my chest and slapping my arms to make sure I was awake, not dreaming. I thought to myself that it would be so easy to go home and pretend nothing had happened. Jack could call his friends and maybe go out with them that evening and I could lie down in my bed and sleep. However, I knew this would not be the right thing to do, so instead I continued to drive around town trying to think think think about where to go.

Jack was getting testy. He hadn't slept in three days. He wanted to go home and take a shower, unpack his bags, and he promised we could rest a little and make an appointment to see a doctor the next morning. It sounded like such a good idea, very logical, I thought, but I knew it wouldn't work. I figured I had one shot at getting this right or Jack would be gone, he would jump out of the car and run off with his ear pressed against his phone calling anyone and everyone to come rescue him and I would never see him again.

So instead I drove straight to what I thought was the mental health hospital, which was in the same complex as the Children's Recovery Center where Jack spent ten days back in September. Along the side of the building I saw a big red sign that said "Admissions" with an arrow pointing the way, and so I parked the car and we followed the directions around the side of the building where we found an unmarked metal door.

"We'll try this, and if it isn't the right place, I'm going home," Jack said to me.

I knocked on the door since there was no doorbell or buzzer, and a man opened the door several inches and peered out at both of us, then he asked if we were indigent.

I didn't really know what he meant, perhaps because nobody had ever asked me that question before, so I just stood there confused, and then said no.

The man opened the door a bit further and explained that Jack had to go to the hospital, the regular hospital, because only that hospital would accept our insurance. It hadn't occurred to me to go where I had taken Jack for an x-ray when he broke his wrist in middle school. I was crestfallen. This was my one chance to get it right, and I had wasted it by going to the wrong place! I thanked the man and started to turn away, but the man continued to stand there with the door open, eyeing us, then he looked directly at Jack, sadly, and wished us good luck before slowly ticking the door back in place.

As we walked back to the car, I was increasingly nervous about what Jack would do next. I knew he wanted to call off the entire venture, but when I looked at him moving toward the car, I noticed he was suddenly unusually quiet, the first time this entire holiday trip. Something had changed inside of him on the way back to the parking lot. His shoulders were hunched down and he stared at the ground, walking slowly. I tried to walk fast because I was worried that he was plotting an escape, but once we got into the car he seemed resigned to his fate. We drove straight to the hospital in complete silence.

And so it was the late evening and one day after Christmas when we finally staggered into the emergency room after a two day drive from Boston to Norman, Oklahoma. We were disheveled and exhausted, and nobody seemed to care that we had dragged our dog into the waiting room with us. Jack hadn't slept at all in several days, but after we sat down in the waiting area, he seemed to regain a bit of energy and started to plead again—couldn't we just go home for a quick shower, and then, he reasoned, we could return to the emergency room later on, once he tried to sleep a little...would that be OK?

It all sounded so plausible...why not? Neither of us had showered for two days, and the thoughts of my bed waiting for me were like a sweet siren song. Why not let your son take a shower before he is put on a 72-hour hold, why not?

I was just then learning enough to say no, however. I was beginning to understand that going home would be dangerous; a shower would be a risk. Jack was a skillful persuader so everything could unravel before my eyes, I could let it happen, especially since I was so tired. So I tried to steel myself, and instead of letting Jack persuade me to take the dog home, I called a friend to come pick him up and drop him off at our house.

After thirty minutes, Jack was finally taken down the hall for his assessment, where he lay there waiting on a hospital bed while I sat on a swivel office chair outside his room looking around for a doctor to arrive. After fifteen minutes of lying fully clothed and face down on the bed, Jack suddenly sprang up and bolted out of the room and down the hall. I jumped up to call after him while a nurse down the hall spun around in his chair and shouted, "where are you going?"

My son answered that he was looking for a bathroom, and just then a security guard appeared, accompanied Jack down the hall, and then they returned together to the hospital room where the guard remained stationed just outside the doorway.

Back in his room after the bathroom sprint, Jack sprawled on the narrow bed with his arms hanging off the sides and his feet extending past the bottom of the thin crinkly mattress. He turned his head toward the door, and after noticing the security guard lingering nearby he summoned the guard into the room with a wave of his hand. The guard was wearing a plastic badge pinned to his lapel that revealed the name "Michael," which was the same name as Jack's grandfather. The deep significance of this cosmic name-parallel was not lost on Jack, who turned toward me with a knowing smirk as I peered in from the hallway.

"You see?" he whispered loudly toward me,

"he has the same name as Granddad, just like in my dream."

I nodded my head and stood up to wheel my chair down the hall to an empty office where I sat alone, resting my head on an abandoned desk and allowing my eyes to close, knowing that Jack was finally safe. Meanwhile, Jack wanted to talk with the guard about his dreams, and so the guard became Jack's sounding board for the next two hours, sharing personal stories from the dream world while waiting for the doctor to arrive.

Jack had just turned eighteen, so there would be no more children's crisis center for him, no more therapeutic rooms filled with toys and counselors to talk with him in a gentle voice about his feelings, no staff members to play games of ping pong with, no parents sobbing quietly in the foyer, no new friends that he recognized from high school, the same age, recovering from the same illness.

Basically, if you don't get healed in the small window of time before you turn eighteen; if you don't get your shit together while you are still a minor, things can definitely take a turn for the worse, but not always. If there is a security guard who talks to you for two solid hours about your hopes and dreams, or a nurse who brings you a sandwich even if you babble at her, or a doctor who sits in front of a computer screen long past midnight trying to figure out how the spaceship and dream machine tie into all of this, you still have a chance.

The facility where the doctors decided to send Jack was the very same building we had started out at earlier that day. This was a locked crisis center for adults, and included homeless people and drug addicts who exhibited behaviors dangerous enough to be brought in off the streets, and that is definitely saying something because most homeless people are left to wander around without anyone noticing their erratic behavior, until they get arrested for trespassing, that is. A coin is flipped and heads you go to the crisis center, tails you go to jail.

The doctor had already drawn Jack's blood at the hospital and they hadn't found any drugs in his system. I desperately wanted the doctors to find drugs, mainly psychosis-inducing drugs. That way, once the drugs left his body, I reasoned, he would be healed. However, it turned out his psychosis was the drug-free variety.

I slowly packed up the rest of my sandwich while a police officer appeared, handcuffed Jack, and walked him through the hospital foyer and out the door to his waiting police car. I followed along, crossed the parking lot to my car and pulled out of my parking spot and into the exit lane behind the police officer. Driving behind a police officer already makes me nervous, but purposefully following one made me inordinately aware of my two hands on the steering wheel and my foot on the gas pedal and the brake.

We arrived at the mental health complex and parked next to the crisis center. The police officer guided Jack by one of his free elbows around to an entrance located on the side of the building that had a glass double door and a buzzer. The officer pressed the buzzer, the door opened, and he motioned for me to step back while he and Jack entered a tiny foyer that had two dirty plastic chairs sitting in front of a large metal detector positioned in front of a long hallway.

I stood outside the door trying to peer in through the streaks of grime on the glass while the two of them waited together, an awkward pair, until a few minutes later a hunched-down man sauntered into the foyer dragging with him three extra inches of ragged pant hem along the floor. I watched Jack plop down in one of the plastic chairs, which strained under his weight, while the man exchanged a few words with the police officer.

I was still trying to decide what to do when the officer opened the door to leave and saw me standing there. He looked surprised and asked if I wanted to wait inside, if Jack allowed me. Jack heard the request and begrudgingly nodded yes, so I slipped in through the door, which swung shut and locked behind me. Hearing the door click made me start to regret my decision to enter, especially since the moment the police officer left, the man disappeared into the bowels of the building, leaving Jack and me alone there. While we waited, Jack grew more and more offended by the dingy room illuminated only by a long fluorescent tube in the ceiling.

"Why am I here?" he asked me angrily, clearly wishing he hadn't agreed to the long drive back to Oklahoma on Christmas Day, to this bait-and-switch—first it was Santa Claus, and then it was Nurse Ratched.

I suddenly realized how exhausted I was and I sat down in the other plastic chair. I had no answer to give him except to remind him that *One Flew Over the Cuckoo's Nest* was a work of fiction and Nurse Ratched was not a real person, the idea of which he laughed at dismissively.

He then turned to look at me as if he were just seeing me for the first time all day, and I slumped there while he sized me up. He must have come to some internal decision because he told me in an icy voice that I should leave.

Not knowing how to leave, I stood up and called out "excuse me!" through the metal detector, hoping my voice would carry down the empty, dimly lit hall to a person. "Can you let me out?" I called again. I heard footsteps, and saw the man round the corner. This time he was moving quickly as he came down the hall and squeezed around the side of the metal detector, being careful not to trip over the elevated cord that reached across from the machine to a wall outlet.

When he saw both of us standing there, he stopped short and narrowed his eyes, looking first at me and then at Jack, who was staring back at him defiantly.

"How did you get in here?" he said. Before I could explain, he asked, "Did someone transport you over from the center?"

"No, no," I said, suddenly understanding his confusion, "this is my son Jack, the police officer let me in too."

The man looked at Jack for confirmation, but Jack stared straight ahead, refusing to acknowledge either of us while tapping his foot loudly on the floor. The man put his hands on his hips and looked back at me.

It was his turn to size me up, so I stood there in the rumpled Christmas outfit I had put on yesterday morning when we were 1,705 miles away from Oklahoma and reached up to straighten my ponytail that was barely held into place by a rubber band. I hoped the man could tell that, despite my appearance, I was A-OK, but then I looked at Jack and felt a stab of guilt in my heart for thinking such a thing.

I knew, however, that if both of us were stuck there, nobody would get home to feed the dog. I figured that in these types of situations it is usually the scowling one who stays while the smiling one gets to leave, so I offered the man what I hoped was a warm, polite smile.

It wasn't the smile that worked, however, but the fact that he noticed my purse, which I had forgotten I was holding, so I handed it to him and he looked inside, where he found my wallet with my driver's license and a set of car keys. I saw him look at the keys, so I pointed out the glass door to my car that matched the keys, which was thankfully clearly visible from where we stood inside. He reached over to unlock the door with a big set of keys tied to his waist like a prison warden in some movie, and I leaned back to say goodbye to Jack before sliding out the door.

I walked out and across the empty parking lot that was now lit only by the light of the moon to my car and I drove home to my dog standing at the front window waiting for me.

Jack spent the coming days at this crisis center calling all of his friends on the hall phone to pass the time until an angry alcoholic smashed the phone to pieces. Once the phone was broken, Jack had nothing else to do but walk up and down the halls like a caged lion trying to burn off the endless amount of energy coursing through his brain and body.

One evening, he later told me, he had been pacing back and forth along the dimly lit hallway of Ward 200 long after midnight when he encountered a night nurse slumped down in a wooden chair at the end of the hallway, half-sleeping against the wall. Jack paused in front of the nurse, who opened his eyes and turned to look up at Jack solemnly. Then the nurse opened his hand, palm outward, and pointed at the sign posted on the wall behind him.

The sign provided a list of rules and regulations for the center together with the grievance process for patients who wished to file a complaint. No words were exchanged between the nurse and Jack, but Jack detected a hidden message in the eyes of the nurse, so, after reading the sign, he turned around very slowly and shuffled back to his room, convinced that the nurse's gesture was his secret way of encouraging Jack to lead an internal protest against the hospital by documenting the failings of the center and fighting for patients' rights via the grievance process. With this newfound purpose, Jack spent the rest of his endless amount of free time gathering forms, writing long memos in pencil, and threatening to file grievances against a majority of the staff members on the ward.

In this way, one day went by, then two, then five, and then a court date was set and a lawyer magically appeared to represent Jack's interests since Jack wanted to leave the center while his counselor and social worker thought he should be transferred to the psychiatric hospital next door.

On a cold Wednesday morning, the first one after Christmas, I arrived at the center at 8 a.m. to sit with Jack and his court-appointed lawyer at a table in the visitor's foyer waiting for the judge to see us. The lawyer pretended to share an interest in Jack, even letting me know that he had a daughter who went to the same high school. This is when I would normally ask for her name, and perhaps ask if she might know my son, since maybe they are both on the swim team together, but instead I knew to hold my tongue because he was a lawyer and my son was his client, so I just sat there nodding my head up and down as if to say, "Ah yes, I see."

After we finished our small talk, a strained silence fell over us, and the lawyer, whose name I do not remember, soon became restless and turned to me to say "Hopefully this hearing will begin soon because you must certainly have better things to do today."

Thoughts of going to the grocery store or stopping at the post office appeared a distant, grainy image in my mind, as if I were now living in a parallel universe where normal things were no longer normal. I shook my head, perhaps a little too vigorously, and responded that I had nothing better to do. Should I have explained that when one goes to court to see if her son will be transferred to the mental hospital, she clears her schedule for the entire day?

CHAPTER FOUR

Strength

The first time I went to visit Jack at the crisis center did not go as planned. I walked inside the dingy breezeway that led into the visitor's area and tried to shut the double glass doors behind me but they kept flapping open, letting the cold air inside. The next set of glass doors that led into the foyer area were locked by a bolt clearly visible in the gap between the two doors, binding them together. The thick bolt did not prevent the man who entered the breezeway right after me from trying to open the door, however, and as he pulled on the door handle, the twin glass doors rattled in their frames while the bolt strained and pulled slightly from its hinge, fighting to keep the doors closed.

There was no sign anywhere that explained the situation with the locked doors because, unlike a prison, this was a crisis hospital with patients instead of inmates, so although they were supposed to be locked in, it was all very discreet. Therefore, in order to come to this place, we all had to be on the same page together, we all had to know where to turn off Main Street and how to navigate around all the numbered buildings in order to park behind one of them, and we all had to know to walk around from the side and enter the unmarked building at 6 p.m., which was the visiting hour, the information of which was not posted anywhere. Since we were the only two visitors standing in the breezeway, this man and I were not only privy to all of these secrets, but we were also both skipping dinner to be here tonight.

I nodded at the man and turned my attention to the wall on the left side of the breezeway where there was an old black phone with no dial to turn and no buttons to press. Above it was a bulletin board with nothing posted on it, and below it was a narrow counter that clearly served as a trash receptacle for two Styrofoam cups with the remnants of dark liquid inside them, a few crumpled napkins, and several pieces of chewing gum stuck to its surface. Next to the counter was a tattered office chair that had likely been wheeled out from an internal office and abandoned there in the breezeway.

I thought that if I worked here I would slip a trash can next to the counter and maybe I would wipe the counter clean from time to time and I might even add a friendly welcome sign and a potted plant, but probably the potted plant would have cigarette butts stubbed out in its dirt.

But I didn't work there. Instead I tried to figure out how to gain access to the building. While I was doing this, a young doctor wearing scrubs slipped into the breezeway from the parking lot, walked over to the phone and lifted up the earpiece, announced her name, the door buzzed, the lock popped open, and she squeezed her body through the now parted double doors that led inside. She glanced back at me quickly with a look in her eyes that seemed to say, "sorry!" Then she marched through the visiting room and disappeared down the hall while the door bolt popped firmly back into place.

I eased myself down into the office chair, testing it first to make sure the legs were steady. Then I carefully lifted up the earpiece and heard the phone ringing on the other end. I looked through the locked glass doors to follow the sound, and saw movement inside the reception area. A woman suddenly appeared behind the scratched Plexiglas screen above the desk and leaned out toward me holding the earpiece of another black phone, the twin of my phone.

She didn't say anything but looked at me expectantly, so I spoke into the mouthpiece of my phone to ask if I could enter, and I gave her Jack's name and I even added his ward number to show her that I really did know what I was talking about, I was not just a random person but I was a mom and I had been invited here. I waited through her pause, hoping that once she finished consulting the paperwork on her desk, she would let me in.

During this pause, I turned to smile at the man still standing in the breezeway; he was waiting not too close but not too far away from me for his turn on the phone. I saw the receptionist disappear for a moment, and then she reappeared at her desk and picked the phone back up. I stood up to connect eyes with her, waiting for her to buzz me in, but instead she looked past me and told me through the phone that I was not allowed to enter.

I wasn't sure how to respond to this so I thanked her and hung up, and then I stepped away from the phone to let the waiting man try his luck. After a quick call, the receptionist came around from her desk, crossed the visiting room, unlocked the door and opened it about six inches or so, just enough for the man to slip in sideways but not open enough to suggest that I too could come through the doors.

Neither of them looked in my direction while this was taking place, perhaps because the man was embarrassed for me while the receptionist was afraid that if she and I made eye contact I would try to plead with her, and she'd have to say "no," and things might have escalated into me yelling at her or even screaming and pounding on the glass doors. But I wanted to show her that I would not do that, so I stood there with a smile frozen on my face as the man walked inside and the receptionist snapped the bolt back in the lock right in front of me while training her eyes on some object out the window past me.

I saw several patients shuffle slowly into the visiting area, and as I continued to stand there and look through the glass doors, I saw the breezeway man walk up to a woman about his age and they embraced each other. Her eyes were red and swollen from crying and her black mascara was streaked down her face but she smiled broadly at the man and they sat down across from each other at a heavy wooden table.

Next I saw a young man enter the room, sit down at a different table, and hunch over, covering his face with his long hair. Nobody came to visit him that evening. At a third table sat a girl who looked to be Jack's age, rocking back and forth while also waiting for a visitor who never arrived. Later that evening this girl set fire to the women's bathroom in order to convince her doctor to release her, which resulted in her immediate arrest. The announcement of this incident appeared in the local newspaper the next day, but the article made no mention of where the girl got the book of matches she had hidden in her sock. This goes to show you that the police will come and get you even from a crisis center if you do not obey the law while you are psychotic.

So I decided to pick up the phone again, and this time I asked to talk to a nurse. The receptionist agreed and hung up her phone, lifted up the receiver again and pressed several buttons while I sat back down in the chair to wait. A few minutes later I saw a woman walk into the visitor's room, and instead of turning off in another direction, she continued to walk directly toward me with a smile on her face. I had hit the jackpot.

The woman unlocked the door and came out into the breezeway and looked me in the eye and talked to me and explained that Jack couldn't see me because he was a flight risk. He had been going around the building earlier that day testing out all the doors and trying the windows, so he couldn't have visitors for three days. I would have been his only visitor, I thought to myself, but now he was locked inside, likely seething in anger while I stood outside thanking the nurse for the information and turning around to leave.

Just as I began to open the door, the nurse put her hand on my arm and I turned back around to face her. She looked at me kindly and asked "How are you doing with all of this?"

I stood there stunned because nobody had asked me that before. Nurses and doctors steer around me, going back and forth while I stand there awkwardly, sometimes waiting for hours while trying to stay out of their way, all the while showing them that I am on their team, that I am not one of those moms who screams and yells at the doctors and says "you can't keep my son here!" or "I am going to sue you!" but instead I stand there smiling and trying to learn as much as possible so they can see that I can be counted on to provide a good support system for Jack.

The nurse's question was so unexpected and I was so worn down by the day's events that although I tried to smile and say something nice, nothing came out of my mouth. Instead I stood there nodding to assure her that I was fine, but I started to cry, which was exactly what I didn't want to happen because I am supposed to be the strong one, so I quickly pulled myself together and told her I was just extremely tired. I beat a hasty retreat out the door, not looking back.

By this time it was very cold outside, with a wind biting and swirling around me, and a sky that was completely dark. I stumbled to my car in the poorly lit parking lot and opened the door quickly, jumped in, and shut and locked the door. I turned on the heat and sat there with my hands on the steering wheel, not moving, and began to think that what I really should have done in the breezeway was to faint into the floor when the nurse asked me how I was doing.

I could have pretended my soul was floating above me looking down at my body while
watching to see what she would do. She would
probably have regretted asking me that question
because if someone else arrived for visiting hours,
that person would have had to step over my limp
body stretched across the floor in order to get
to the phone above the counter, and then to the
door. Maybe the nurse would have alerted someone inside the hospital, who would send out two
burly men to pick me up and carry me into the
foyer, and they would give me medications to
make me feel far away and hazy before putting
me in bed to sleep. What is so bad about that?

I continued to think this idea through while
my car warmed up in the quiet parking lot.
Instead of going home to my empty house and
doing laundry and finishing my report for work
tomorrow, I thought that I could be sitting on
one of those big cozy couches in the rec room
watching television, maybe shaking a little bit
from my medicine, maybe slightly confused by
what was on the television screen in front of me,
but nobody would care about that, I could think
and say whatever I wanted—as long as I didn't
change the channel.

I then envisioned what would be Jack's surprise when he turned the corner into the rec
room and saw me sitting there, in my hospital-is-
sue pajamas! I would smile really big and scoot

over, patting the cushion next to me.

"To hell with visitor's hours!" I'd say, and he'd plop down on the couch next to me and we'd both giggle together, unless he was mad at me for being there too, taking the wind out of his sails, so-to-speak, which would more likely be the case, so he'd probably just scowl at me and storm out of the room.

Soon, however, dinner would be served, so I'd jump up from the couch, or maybe I would stand up slowly, depending on how my medicine was affecting me, and I'd shuffle into the dining room, where a buffet table lined the far wall with a row of those big rectangular food bins set above warming trays.

The buffet table would have a hood above it with plastic screens coming down the sides to protect the food from coughs and sneezes, and I'd have to bend my knees a bit in order to reach under the hood to fill my plate. I would scan the tables for Jack, trying to find a seat not too close but not too far from him while making sure not to look at his plate to see if he had chosen a side vegetable, because now he is an adult and I am trying really hard not to be a helicopter mom.

My thoughts shifted to an image of the snarly staff woman who sat in the corner of the visiting room at the recovery center where my son was hospitalized earlier in the fall. She stayed there, perched precariously on a narrow stool throughout all the visiting hours, where she would make a point of looking at each child with disgust as they shuffled past her with downcast eyes. One boy's parents brought cookies for their son, and when he tried to share them with Jack the woman became enraged and ordered the boy back to his seat. No parents ever spoke up, clearly for fear of retaliation.

It occurred to me that maybe a surly staff woman worked at this crisis center too, and when I slid my feet along to the buffet table she might look at me in the same hateful way. However, I would take my cue from the other patients and keep my mouth shut, but my eyes wide open. Then, I'd spend the rest of my time in the hospital scouring all of the staff areas each day for a book of matches so that I, too, could set the bathroom on fire. During the resulting melee I would run down the hall toward my son's ward, turn breathlessly into his room, and if he happened to be asleep, I would throw him over my shoulder and run as fast as I could to the exit, making sure his long legs didn't drag on the ground. The problem is, I am not sure what I'd do next.

———————

Before I shifted my car into drive I had to wipe the condensation off the windows with the sleeve of my jacket. I steered out of the parking lot, still thinking about that woman. I hoped that nobody in this hospital would look at Jack in that mean way, and instead he would get to talk to the kind nurse who came out into the foyer, and maybe someone would give him a hug before he went to bed.

I finally pulled into my driveway, pressed the button to open my garage door, and staggered into my kitchen. A headache had crept up on me during the drive home so I took a bottle of aspirin out of the pantry and stumbled through the house in the dark and down the hall to my bedroom, where I pulled off my shoes and climbed into my bed fully dressed. It was still a bit early and I had a report due at the office tomorrow, but I was too tired to think about working on it, so I set my alarm clock back an hour to allow time to finish the report in the morning. Then I sat up against my pillow and held my aching head in my hands, wondering what my next move should be. I am the one who has to keep the boat afloat, I thought to myself, so I needed all my strength. Most importantly, though, I needed to sleep, but that wasn't happening.

Across my dark bedroom, my dresser mirror reflected a blade of light coming through the slats of my window blind from the streetlamp outside that danced across the opposite wall in horizontal strips of light. I squinted at the light then closed my eyes as the brightness cut into me. I covered my eyes with my hands and wondered how light can have such a sharp, palpable presence. After a while I lay down and tossed and turned until I was finally able to fitfully fall asleep.

CHAPTER FIVE

The Hermit

The judge concurred with the counselor and social worker that Jack should be transferred to the mental health hospital next door, so the morning after his hearing, the lengthy release and re-admittance process began. It started in the morning with the nurse, who spent her time filling out all the medical and legal paperwork, collecting all the necessary signatures, and filing all the forms away into cabinets. Full accounting was made of all of Jack's possessions, from the things he arrived with that he could not keep in his room to the clothing and books he accumulated from various visitors he had received while in the crisis center. All these things were categorized, labeled, written out on a list and checked off the list, placed in plastic bags, and brought out into the foyer.

Jack sat in the foyer another hour waiting while a bedroom at the hospital was made ready for him. While he sat there, a man wheeled across the foyer in an old, rickety wheelchair. He was missing one leg, his clothing was ragged, and he appeared not to have bathed in quite some time, given the sharp odor of stale urine that followed after him. His hair and beard were both filthy. Jack glanced over at him and then looked back at me.

"He's homeless," Jack said by way of explanation as he jerked his head toward the man. "He checks himself in to the center every time the weather gets too cold."

"Why doesn't he go to the shelter?" I asked, and Jack shrugged his shoulders. "He's an alcoholic," he responded.

Next, a teenage girl meandered into the foyer and looked around before spotting her mother, who was pacing back and forth arguing with someone on the phone. The girl was being released today as well, but she was going home rather than to the hospital. Her mother looked up from her angry phone conversation and saw her daughter standing there.

"Where are all your things?" she asked impatiently.

"I need to get the luggage cart to carry everything," responded the daughter.

She turned on her heels, cast her mother a sideways glance and sauntered over to a brass cart, a hand-me-down of the kind used at nice hotels that seemed to have appeared out of nowhere. She tugged on the handle and the cart started moving across the foyer in slow motion until the girl disappeared down the hall, the cart rolling behind her. I looked over at her mother, who, having ended her phone conversation, stood there expressionless and rooted in the same spot absentmindedly twirling car keys in her hand.

About fifteen minutes later the girl emerged again, this time with several large plastic bags, pillows and boxes stacked on the cart that she slowly wheeled toward her mother. Both mother and daughter walked toward the door together, looking completely bored as if a haze had engulfed both of them. As an afterthought, the mother said, "I'll go get the car." The daughter pulled the cart to a halt and stood by the door waiting.

Just then, two guards came through the double doors and brushed past the girl, one carrying a set of handcuffs. They stopped and looked over at Jack, who was seated at a table busily reviewing a set of printouts that explained in elementary terms the different mental diagnoses, what prescriptions Jack could expect to take, and what side effects he should anticipate. He had a pencil tucked behind his ear and a sheet of paper ready to take notes at his exit meeting, but they weren't needed since there was no exit meeting, no nurse, no doctor, and no farewells, just the appearance of the guards to signal that his time here was over. Upon seeing the guards, Jack stood up and held his arms behind his back so they could put the handcuffs around his wrists. A seasoned handcuff wearer, I thought to myself.

The girl, still hanging by the door, observed this interaction and looked at Jack with a heightened level of interest as she tried to size up the situation. Her previously dull eyes sparkled with admiration as she watched the guards step on either side of my now-shackled son, each holding an arm with a light bit of pressure, and in that way the three of them walked past the girl and through the double doors like a set of triplets. On their way out, the girl turned to Jack and asked "Who are you, the badass?" then she cackled to expose a set of perfect white teeth. Jack passed by without glancing her way, instead he looked straight ahead while walking through the doors that promptly slammed behind him, cutting off any further commentary.

I knew that the air hit Jack's face just outside the door because I could see him draw in his breath. He took one brief look back through the now closed glass doors and smirked at the girl before pausing for a moment to look around. He hadn't really known what the outside of the building looked like in daylight, so the guards kindly waited while Jack stood there a moment, inhaling fresh air. The crisis center had no slightly open windows, no concrete-lined outside courtyard, and no fenced-in yard with dirt to walk around, so Jack had breathed only stale ventilated air for five days. He knew he had just a short walk because the hospital was right next door so he tried to stroll slowly in order to lengthen the brief time he had outside. Almost as soon as he was outside, though, he was back inside, where his paperwork was processed and he was taken to his new room to unpack his possessions and start a new daily schedule of waiting to get better.

This hospital was an improvement over the crisis center in that it didn't have any broken windows or wobbly chairs. The tight entrance room opened up into a larger interior, with a series of small spaces with narrow halls that branched off into stuffy, windowless offices and lab rooms. The dining room also doubled as the visiting room and looked more like a small classroom with its plastic chairs lined up alongside the rows of long tables. Jack had more free time to explore this hospital, so I brought him books to read and spiral-free notebooks to write in with different colors of thin washable markers. In the evenings, Jack would wander up and down the halls of his ward, all alone, trying to assess his situation and make sense of what was happening to him.

———————

It was at this hospital where Jack first began to notice that everywhere he looked, he saw the names of pharmaceutical drugs written on all the objects in the hospital. This medical branding began with the short films that Jack was required to watch during his stay, films that provided a generic overview of mental illness. It reminded me of Friday movie night at college, which was always attended by the students who didn't have cars, money, or friends. Jack sat next to the other patients, each one slumping as if it took every last bit of energy to balance his heavy head on his neck.

At the end of the commercialized films, the names of the sponsoring drug companies rolled up in the credits in a list that extended longer than the movies had. The films introduced the patients to a new vocabulary: Paxil Zoloft Celexa Effexor Wellbutrin Elavil Lexapro Ativan Xanax Buspar Abilify Risperdal Zyprexa Seroquel and Geodon. While all the side effects of these medications were carefully explained, their benefits were never fully discussed.

After the first movie night, Jack the noctambulist returned to his room but was unable to sleep, so he began to pace the halls of the wards at night, and it was then that he started to notice how these pharmaceutical names also appeared everywhere in the hospital—on the walls, on objects, in every room. As he walked around the ward that first night, he noticed in the dim, blinking fluorescent light of 4 a.m. that the hall clocks all ticked Zyprexa with their tick-tock plastic arrow hands lurching around the circle of time, slow and steady. In the nurses' stations, wall calendars behind the Plexiglas spoke of Xanax, with their appointments neatly written into the small squares of time that were arranged into four rows of seven boxes. Round pencil holders stood patiently nearby, waiting to help out, while boldly appealing to Adderall to keep things focused and in order.

When he went to his doctor's appointment the next day, Jack noticed that the doctor's notepads loudly announced Haldol Haldol Haldol in a slow rhythm to drown out the cacophony of internal voices, while pens quietly scribbled Seroquel and mouse pads optimistically promised Paxil and Prozac. Every time the doctor reached for a cup of coffee, his mug whispered Risperdal, each sip a gentle reminder to replenish the stock of name-brand medications. At least the coffee cup didn't advertise the sleep aid Lunesta, although the irony might have been appreciated. Generic brands were nowhere to be seen. And so it was in this hospital that Jack first learned to fight back against this insidious "Big Pharma" advertising by slipping his pills beneath the sofa cushions directly in front of the surveillance cameras, which earned him a longer hospital stay.

Christmas seemed like a distant memory now that New Year's Eve had come and gone with no celebrations, week one, week two, and then Jack was released back into the world. Now it was Depakote, 500 mgs twice a day, Zyprexa, 15 mgs at night, and Celexa, 20 mgs in the morning. Jack's healthcare plan was to exercise, maintain a regular bedtime, eat healthy food and avoid drugs, alcohol, caffeine and sugar. But Jack does none of these things. With aggressive treatment, 30% of all patients will not have another recurrence of psychosis, but that will not be Jack.

CHAPTER SIX

Nine of Swords

It was 3:02 a.m. and I lay in bed with my head resting on a flat pillow and my comforter pulled up under my chin. I tried to stay asleep but my brain kept clicking on and introducing new thoughts that kept me awake. This particular night I was thinking about my 10 a.m. meeting at work and how I needed to leave early to get Jack to his 11 a.m. doctor's appointment. I had already picked out a chair in the back of the conference room that was closest to the side exit, but I had to make sure I got to the meeting early enough to claim that seat, which meant I would have to cut my 9 a.m. artist interview short by ten minutes so I could run directly over to the building.

Also, if I were lucky, no one would see me leave, so I wouldn't have to explain why I needed to go to the doctor's office so much. It would be like an early lunch, I thought to myself, which reminded me that I wouldn't have time to eat, so

I reached across my bed to the side table where my clock now glowed 3:17 a.m. and I used the light on my phone to see which buttons to press to set my alarm clock back ten minutes in order to have time to pack a lunch.

Jack wanted to go out for lunch after his appointment, but he had already missed so many classes that I needed to drive him straight back to school, and in my mind's eye I could already see him pouting angrily while clutching the crinkled yellow doctor's note I hoped he would remember to give the school secretary because he was at the end of his allowed number of absences and he really needed to graduate from high school.

I twisted around under my blanket, not comfortable. It was now 3:33 a.m. and I reached across to set my alarm clock back five more minutes to make sure I had enough time to make a sandwich for Jack too. I lay back down again, nestling my head into my pillow, and tried to breathe deeply and smoothly while willing the beats of my heart to slow down. I still couldn't sleep. I tried counting to see if I could banish the thoughts from my brain, but the internal chatter instead shifted to the artist interview I had scheduled for first thing in the morning. I would have to drop Jack off at school a bit earlier in the morning so I could get to work with enough time to set up the recording equipment, which never seemed to work for me, and if I needed to call the IT guy, I'd have to do that by 8:30 a.m. At 8:15, however, I knew I would still be home listening to Jack construct an argument for why he should be allowed to stay home until his doctor's appointment.

I tried not to peek at my clock again but I couldn't stop myself, so I opened my eyes very slightly to see that it was now 3:47 a.m. If Jack would just graduate from high school, I thought, things would get better because I knew he would love college and would want to study and learn. I tried to convince myself that it was just high school that was the problem, and it would soon be over if only I could get Jack out of bed and into the classroom.

My thoughts drifted again, this time to an image of Jack sleeping in his bed. Perhaps he was awake too, lying in a bed identical to mine but separated from me by three walls and two doors. I suddenly felt a rush of fear tingle beneath my skin, and the parts of my body that I had shuttered down while trying to rest were now wide-awake. I had a mental image of Jack's bed, empty, and the screen torn off his bathroom window. Just the other morning I had found his screen hidden behind a pile of clothing in his closet, so I knew the window was the escape route that allowed him to sneak out of the house without the dog barking.

On previous nights, however, I was bliss-fully unaware of this tactic and I didn't hear his comings and goings, nor even if anyone else was in my house during the night, I had been sleeping so peacefully. Now I was not, however. If he sneaked out tonight, I wondered, what would I be able to do? Call him on his cell phone and ask him where he was? "Look, my mom is calling, ha!" he would say to his friends and they would all laugh while he clicked his phone off. So no, I could do nothing. Was it better not to know? I had been trying not to think negative thoughts, but they kept flooding into my brain uninvited, so maybe not knowing was better, I decided.

It then occurred to me, however, that if I did check on him and he was asleep, I would have a better chance of falling asleep myself. With that, I got out of bed, grabbed my phone from my bedside table, and used it to illuminate my way down the hall and across the living room to Jack's bedroom, where I slowly pushed the door open and crept over to his bed, hoping my phone light would not meet the whites of his eyes staring back at me, simmering with anger at this breach of privacy. That would be confirmation I was the crazy one, creeping around the house at night, in the dark, spying.

His bedroom curtains were open and moonlight was filtering into the room at soft angles, so I turned my phone light off. In the dim light I saw Jack lying across his bed on his stomach with his head turned sideways, his eyes closed, and his long arms and legs splayed across the top of the comforter. He was still wearing his clothing.

His hands were at his sides with his palms facing down, so I could see the geometric patterns he had drawn on them with a thin black indelible marker. A few months ago he had started experimenting with lucid dreaming and drew a small triangle on the back of his left hand that functioned as a dreaming reminder. Throughout the day, he would look at the symbol and confirm that he was awake. Once he fell asleep, he could look at his hand and ask the same question, and if the symbol was either gone or altered in some way, it meant to him that he was dreaming. Soon he began to draw the small triangle slightly larger, and he added either a circle or a square inside the triangle—these were the three universal shapes, according to Leonardo da Vinci.

Every few days Jack would retrace the outline of these symbols with his black marker, and over time the images became more elaborate. More recently he had also started drawing thin lines down the inside of each finger, following the direction of his bones, so his hands were covered in linear patterns of black ink like a strange inversion of some Australian aboriginal x-ray painting.

As I stood over his bed, I noticed that six inches away from his decorated left hand was his cell phone lying on a pillow, and his arm was stretched toward it in his sleep with his hand poised ready to answer any late night messages. He wouldn't have wanted to miss any action, I thought. I looked down at the phone, which was facing upward on his bed, and even though he kept his phone locked, I knew that if I pressed the screen button I could illuminate the list of caller's names and the times of their messages.

I looked over at Jack's face, half of which was barely visible while the other half was bathed in moonlight. I wondered what would happen if he woke up right now. I slowly reached toward his phone, stretching my body precariously across the bed. My fingers groped for the small, cold metal surface and I pressed the round button at the bottom of the screen. The screen lit up in an eerie blue glow:

Message from Sarah, 1:59 a.m.

Snapchat from Caitlyn 2:15 a.m.

Message from Noah, 3 a.m.

Message from Noah, 3:15 a.m.

Message from Noah, 3:17 a.m.

I noticed this last message was a little less than thirty minutes ago, and Jack must have fallen asleep sometime before the 1:59 a.m. call since none of them appeared to have been answered. I clicked the button on the screen again to turn the light off while wondering what was going on with his friend Noah. Maybe he was bored and couldn't sleep on a school night, or maybe his car was in a ditch somewhere and he didn't want to tell his parents. My heart fluttered at that thought.

Since I was already leaning across the bed and pressing the front of the phone, I turned my head slightly and eased my body over to the right just a bit in order to be closer to Jack's face. His face was that of an angel, so calm and relaxed in such a deep sleep—he was dead asleep, I heard myself think, which suddenly made my stomach churn in fear.

Then my initial relief that Jack was home asleep rather than out the bedroom window turned into a sudden bit of panic as I wondered why I couldn't hear his breathing, nor was his body moving at all—no light snoring, no curling his arms around his pillow with his sleeping fingers fluttering, no slight twitching while I stood over him. I leaned my head right above his chest, careful not to touch him, but just close enough to see if his rib cage was rising up and down with the movement of air in and out of his lungs.

I looked at Jack's arms reaching across the bed stiffly and back to his torso just in time to see what I thought was the slightest movement of his breath. I trained my eyes on a spot on his back that was visible in the dim moonlight of his room until I could see the writing on his shirt move up and down, then again, ever so slightly.

Suddenly he snored once, gently, which startled me almost into laughter. I was relieved to know that, despite everything, on this particular night, Jack was home sleeping soundly. I felt as if I had been given a reprieve, and now I could breathe too. I eased up from his bed and inched carefully out of his room and back to my bedroom, where I lay down in my bed, finally exhausted. I checked my clock one final time—it was now 4:15 a.m., and I could sleep for exactly three hours before my alarm clock woke me.

My mind wandered once more before falling asleep. Just that afternoon Jack told me he would rather have cancer, and I wondered if I agreed with him. I guess it would depend on the type of cancer, I thought. Or else something like my neighbor, who is missing an arm, the result of a farming accident when he was young. One day my neighbor showed me how his mechanical arm couldn't even hold a pencil, it kept slipping through the rubbery fingers. We were both laughing while watching the pencil fall to the ground. My neighbor was originally right-handed, he explained, but after the accident he didn't want to work on his father's farm so he learned how to write with his left hand and applied to college.

He was always so happy, and from that I

concluded that missing an arm was "hands down" preferable to my son's illness, no pun intended. My God, this was a ridiculous idea, I thought, while trying to catch my ragged breathing and force my brain to move in a different direction—to sheep jumping over a white picket fence, one after another, with a beautiful pasture behind them.

The sound of my alarm clock woke me from my short but deep sleep, and as I sat up in bed I had already made the decision to take Jack out to a nice lunch after his doctor's appointment because who really cares about another unexcused absence from school.

Winter gradually turned into spring, and nights and days were filled with sleep, school, Zyprexa titrated down, Celexa titrated up, before Jack started hiding his medicine. Jack had one remaining high school class required for graduation, so each morning I would drag him out of bed and drive him over to school so he could complete a word search or worksheet, and then he would rest his head on his desk for the remainder of the class time, thereby receiving the coveted attendance grade. He still managed to miss so many days of school, however, that I was reduced to digging through his backpack to salvage as many wrinkled doctor's notes as I could and turn them in to the secretary so he wouldn't exceed the state-allotted number of absences allowed for graduation.

In this way, the spring semester came to an end and students began to prepare for high school graduation. I purchased the necessary cap and gown, paid for all the lost library books, and looked over his transcript again and again to make certain he would indeed be walking up the aisle from his alphabetically designated tenth-row seat to collect his soft diploma cover and tassel.

The evening of graduation arrived without much planning, and Jack and I drove over to the auditorium in silence. During the ceremony I could see Jack sitting in his black metal folding chair with his head hanging down; he was clearly not buying the story the valedictorian expounded upon about the new life chapter each student was embarking upon, the earnest love they all felt for each other, and the utmost respect they had for their alma mater. At the end of the ceremony, all the laughter and the hugs and kisses were carefully documented with photographs to prove these sentiments were true, but neither Jack nor I took any photographs on that day.

CHAPTER SEVEN

Justice

Jack had one more thing to take care of before graduation, however—he needed to go to court. After Jack's DUI in the fall of his senior year, I knew I had to get him a lawyer but I wasn't sure of how to go about finding one, except to leaf through the phonebook, which I did in late October after he was released from the crisis center and we had returned from his first college visit. In this way I found the name of a local attorney, and I went to visit her to tell her the story of Jack.

This attorney was very young, and when she stood up to shake my hand I saw that she was wearing a beautiful red sweater and pearls, a tight heather-gray skirt, and black high-heeled shoes with pointed toes. I figured that anyone capable of wearing stiletto heels to court without falling down was the right choice for Jack, so I hired her on the spot.

Then we waited. We waited through the winter and spring for something to happen. We waited until May, just before high school graduation, when Jack was summoned to court, which required him to miss yet another day of school. I knew not to expect a phone call or a notice in the mail about his court appearance because Jack's lawyer had told me that people are supposed to look on the computer every day to see the upcoming docket, that is, if they have a computer and know where the website is, which is tricky because nobody but lawyers know this information. Jack's lawyer checked the docket every morning so she would know when to call us, and then she probably ran home to change into her heels so that she would be dressed nicely for court.

As for us, it didn't seem to matter what we were doing, if we were traveling somewhere or going to school, if we were at work on that day or home sick. We learned that when your case is set on the docket, you have to be in the courtroom at the appointed hour with your lawyer and wearing your best outfit. Then you have to wait and wait in the back of the room, and you'd better not need to go to the bathroom because if you slip out and they call your name, the judge will issue a warrant for your arrest while you are sitting on the toilet, and the court officer will wait outside the bathroom stall until you flush and then you can wash your hands before he shows you the warrant and you are handcuffed.

Instead, we sat in the back of the courtroom holding in our pee, prepared to face the judge so Jack could tell him in a calm and intelligent manner how he was OK, even though he wasn't OK. The main thing I knew, however, was that Jack's statement needed to be short! I explained to him before we arrived that brevity was more important than guilt or innocence in the courtroom because the docket was long and everybody wanted to be home for dinner. So we sat waiting, not squirming at all but trying to remain silent.

I looked around to see a room full of people who were sad or hurt or sick and had families to feed and bills to pay but were having trouble following the rules. Who could remember all the rules, given that our civil law code in the state of Oklahoma ran 592,000 pages, so why not just forget about it all, kick back and smoke a spliff?

On the far side of the room was a boy about Jack's age, slumped down on a wooden bench that spanned the length of three rows of chairs. He was half lying down and half sitting up, not quite tired or awake enough to commit to either option. He didn't seem to have any parents or a lawyer present. I looked across the room to see a group of court-appointed lawyers standing around sifting through files in a cardboard box trying to match up the folders with the people in the courtroom.

One of these lawyers must have been representing the boy, I thought, but nobody was sitting with the boy in the way that Jack's lawyer was sitting with us; instead all these lawyers were glancing around the room casually as if it were all no big deal and one of them said something I couldn't hear and they all laughed a little bit together. My lawyer didn't look over to acknowledge any of them, but I did, and then I looked back at the boy to see his eyes slowly starting to close as his head began to tilt down toward the bench.

I felt sorry for him and I imagined getting up and walking across the courtroom with my arms open so I could give him a big hug and tell him that somebody loved him very much—but I didn't know if that were true or not, maybe nobody loved him, with his soft brown doe eyes—so instead I thought that I would tell him to sit up straight because "You have self-worth and you are not alone," to which he would likely have responded, "Don't touch me, you crazy bitch!"

I looked back at Jack, and at that moment the judge called us up to the bench. The judge was now saying something and I nodded my head in agreement, and my lawyer joined me in nodding her head, the two of us flanking Jack with our wisdom and good judgment. The judge deferred

Jack's sentence, assigned him fees and fines, community service, DUI classes, and probation. We thanked him profusely and headed over to the jail for processing, where I was directed to sit in the lobby while Jack was taken through a set of windowless double metal doors and into a room to sit for 45 minutes until someone sauntered into the room and motioned him over to the counter where he was fingerprinted and photographed.

Meanwhile I sat in the lobby distractedly wondering if his mug shot looked OK, given that he was wearing his good suit and tie. The photo would be a frontal, half-length formal portrait that probably looked better than his senior photos, which I didn't think turned out very well. I wondered if I could buy copies of Jack's mug shot, thinking that if I could just trim off the bottom where he was holding the identification plaque, we could submit it to his high school yearbook. Who would know? Just then Jack came back out through the metal doors and walked toward me, ready to go. We both wanted to leave before we saw anyone we knew, so I grabbed my bag and we fast-walked out the door.

The next thing was the paperwork. Since I didn't know what paperwork was important and what wasn't, I photocopied everything in triplicate and made sure never to give away my originals. That was tricky because everyone who signed and stamped these forms wanted to keep the originals, so I had to be very clever about who got what since now we were playing a ruthless game of bureaucracy where a paperwork failure meant a jail sentence, beginning with the initial receipt of court costs paid to the court clerk right after we left the courtroom that day to the fees paid to the District Attorney's Office the following month to the letter waiving all subsequent fines pursuant to Jack's completion of high school, the transcript of which he had to bring to the judge in June.

There was the letter that gave the date and time of the initial processing by the probation officer, a day and time that Jack could not miss even though he didn't even know what day it was. Once the probation meetings were set up, I kept a list of all subsequent appointments and paid all the related fees, the receipts of which I kept in my folder. Still, this was more than a test of memory and money, it was also a test of logistics because now all the people with DUIs who had lost their licenses needed rides everywhere to get all of their paperwork done, and in Jack's case, I was that driver.

Next was the substance abuse assessment, and since Jack answered all the questions honestly, the report was grim, with a recommendation for the same in-patient treatment that he was just released from before he went to court. I suggested to Jack that he repeat the test with the goal of appearing well enough to merit the lowest level of paperwork and the ten-hour weekend driving class since he won't be driving anyway given that I can't afford the newly priced car insurance with his name listed on it as a high risk driver, so he did that and passed the test. He attended a victim's impact panel where he received a beautiful certificate of completion on nice thick paper with a fancy embossed seal that looked better than his high school diploma. Both of these forms had to be delivered to the instructor of the DUI class, who, at the end of the class, printed off a certificate of completion that was signed and stamped in red ink only.

All these pieces of paper went back to the lawyer. She also received copies of the letters attesting to the completion of the volunteer hours selected from the places on the approved list that were printed off and handed to him at court.

The list included sweeping the office where he went for his probation meetings to helping move the large tables from one end of the cafeteria to the other at the food pantry, so he completed one hour of work in each place that was carefully written on the approved sheet of paper and stamped. Thirty-eight more hours to go.

I noticed that while there seemed to be much work that needed to be done at parks, hospitals, schools and nursing homes around town, none of those types of places were on the list, so instead Jack spent his time washing the car of the security guard at the shopping mall and gathering balls at the golf course until one day he received an updated volunteer list that included an animal shelter.

"Maybe the list is so small because people are afraid to have someone like me work for them," Jack said, with a worried look on his face.

Since the animals wouldn't judge him, nor would animals try to clip him with golf balls like the tan-khakied and pink-collared men at the golf course, he decided to complete the rest of his hours at the shelter.

"Maybe they'll let me walk some of the dogs," he wondered.

"I'm not sure they even take them on walks," I countered, but when we pulled into the parking lot one Saturday afternoon, two women were standing in front of the shelter, each with an eager dog attached to a leash.

We walked into the foyer and Jack handed his court-ordered volunteer sheet to the receptionist, who snapped open the ledger for him to sign in, and she handed him a bucket and mop and directed him down the back hall. This is when Jack discovered where all the sick animals are kept—they are in the back room lying in their own vomit, crying and whining, desperately scratching their mangy skin.

It makes sense—the well-behaved, clean and cute dogs and cats got to lounge in the front cages waiting to be adopted and the most special dog of all was allowed to lie on a plump cushion right behind the receptionist's desk while the damaged, unadoptable animals sat in the back room waiting to die.

The stench in the back room was so unbearable that Jack fought to keep from retching while he mopped the floor in front of the cages, wringing the mop out in the bucket and trying not to slosh water on his face. That is where I found him three hours later, standing in the back room clutching a bucket of feces with tears rolling down his cheeks. His face was streaked brown where the dust hanging in the air met the moisture that clung to his face.

He put the bucket down and tried to wipe his eyes but his sleeves were damp from sweat and his hands were filthy, so he wiped his face and hands with a paper towel and together we walked down the hall toward the reception area where we could see two older women, regular volunteers at the shelter, chatting with a family interested in adopting a dog.

"This one is a miniature schnauzer, we call him Benjamin. He barks at strangers, but is very good with children," one of the women explained. Benjamin turned to us with his tongue lolling out the side of his mouth, and I thought I saw him wink at me very slowly.

"This one is adorable," the mother of the

family cooed, petting a female yorkie while a large black lab waited patiently next to the other volunteer, wagging his tail.

"I just brought this lab back from his walk," the woman offered, leading him over to the family.

"It's so nice that you volunteer here," the father said, smiling broadly at the two women.

At that moment Jack and I entered the reception area and walked diagonally through the foyer toward the exit. It was that precise moment the smell hit me, the smell that had followed us from the back room and clung persistently to Jack's clothing and hair, the smell that began to pervade my clothing by proximity. The odor began to fill the foyer, and in this way it arrived at the nostrils of the two volunteers and all the family members, each of them breathing in the stink simultaneously. All of them turned to look at us with variations on the theme of extreme aversion unfolding across their faces. I looked sideways and stiffly nodded hello while Jack stared straight at the exit with a laser focus. We walked through the door, out into the fresh air, got into the car quickly, and drove home in silence with the windows rolled down.

The following Thursday Jack returned to work at the shelter, and when he finished his four-hour shift, he handed his volunteer sheet to the young man who was working at the receptionist desk, and when Jack asked him to sign and stamp his volunteer sheet, the man thought a moment, sighed, and signed and stamped all the remaining hours Jack needed to work, eight hours total. In that way Jack was officially done with his court-ordered volunteer hours.

With this part of Jack's sentence completed, we gathered together all the volunteer paperwork and brought it to the lawyer's office and she made copies, signed some additional forms, and then all this paper traveled from the lawyer's office to the office of the court clerk in a steady stream where the court clerk stamped each piece of paper and sent individual letters back to both Jack and his lawyer confirming receipt of the completion of the paperwork for each part. All this duplication calmed my nerves because, I reasoned, if my house burned to the ground, I'd still have proof that all of Jack's forms had been completed so nobody could come for him with a warrant to arrest him for the crime of violating the terms of his paperwork.

I thought again about the sleepy boy in court that day, the boy with the doe eyes who probably didn't ever have a ride anywhere to do his volunteer hours, nor any help completing his paperwork. His court forms were likely not photocopied in triplicate, nor arranged neatly in a thick folder sitting on his desk together with receipts of all the payments somebody made on his behalf.

Then I thought about my own sleepy boy, lying in his bed staring up at the ceiling while I made dinner. He did not care at all about any of this.

CHAPTER EIGHT

The Emperor (reversed)

The door jingled as I walked through it into the waiting room of the court services building. A week after Jack's court date, he started his supervised probation meetings. I had come to pick him up but he remained seated in one of the metal folding chairs that lined the far wall, still waiting for his appointment. I glanced over to where he sat hunched forward pretending to read a book as if he were at the doctor's office while at the same time trying to appear nonchalant in the gray area between his mother on one side of the room near the entrance and a group of people on probation leaning against the wall on the opposite side of the room.

Being very careful not to acknowledge Jack, I turned to the desk and paid the first installment of his monthly probation fees and pocketed the receipt the receptionist carefully wrote out for me. I glanced down at the sheet on her desk to make sure Jack had signed in, and then I sat down in one of the chairs next to the receptionist's desk across from where everyone else was waiting and I pulled out my own book to read. So there we were, two seemingly unrelated people sitting across from each other in the waiting room of the court services building, both reading Kurt Vonnegut—what are the statistical chances of that happening?

Finally Jack's name was called by a disembodied voice projecting out from one of the several rooms lining the hallway that grew out from the waiting room. I flinched and looked over at him sharply to make sure he heard his name and claimed his identity without delay because every time a name was called out, the ever-expanding group of waiting people shifted and shuddered in unison while they looked around to eyeball the namee, ready to jump the line in front of anyone who hesitated. Jack must have heard his name because he looked up for a moment and carefully folded down the page that begins Chapter 30 of Vonnegut's *Slapstick*. He casually stood, stretched, and headed down the hall where he turned left and disappeared through his probation officer's door.

I looked up from my seat and watched him walk down the hallway. I wanted so badly to be a fly on the wall in that room so I could hear what the probation officer asked Jack and

I could know how Jack responded and I could see if the officer was kind and asked Jack about his life or if Jack just sat there silently while the man, who was maybe a women, took a cursory glance at him and then spent the rest of the time clacking on his/her computer keyboard, squinting at the screen while filling out the spaces that popped up on the form, trying to squeeze all the letters of Jack's name into the narrow box in order to confirm that he had indeed showed up for his appointment.

I was certain that Jack would also not be looking kindly at the probation officer, nor seeking some sort of human connection. He would be slumped down in his chair waiting waiting and not talking because what is there to say anyway while the officer finished the form with an electronic signature, printed it off and handed it to Jack to deliver to the receptionist at the front entrance, who would stamp the form and slip it into a folder in the low metal file cabinet behind her, right below the sign that listed contact information for "felon-friendly" employers.

If I were a fly, I thought, I would coast into the building through the front door that was always left hanging open and I would slowly circle around the outer hallway, gliding along just a few inches below the asbestos ceiling tiles, and I would be careful not to get near the long fluorescent lights that lined the center of the hallway ceiling with hot white tubes glowing in their metal hoods.

I leaned away from my chair to stare up at the dark stains formed from the dampened ceiling tiles that had rusted the metal clamps holding the lights in place, and then I looked at the glass tubes struggling to keep from flickering on and off above a man pacing in the hallway with an angry scowl on his face.

I calculated that as a fly, I would have to stay above that man's arm's reach, so I would need to make slow, silent circles in the hallway corner while waiting to hear Jack's name being called, and then, upon hearing it, I would hover in the air until he walked out of the waiting room, and I would fall in line behind him and we would move together down the hall while I made sure to stay a comfortable distance above him so he wouldn't notice I was there. When he turned to enter the room, I would bank right the way airplanes do and silently but quickly cut closer to him, accelerating slightly to make sure I got into the room before Jack shut the door behind him.

Once in the room, I would land on something up high where people couldn't reach me even with a fly swatter, so maybe I'd land on the top of a bookshelf, if there is one, and then I'd try to stay very still, although I imagined that this must be very hard for flies to do. So once I landed on top of the bookshelf, I would focus on trying not to totter around too much on my skinny black stick legs that folded out at odd angles.

I would also have to make sure not to be too distracted by the large particles of dust the size of basketballs all around me because they would actually be pretty interesting to look at from up close with my huge bug eyes that functioned as a combination of a kaleidoscope and a microscope, and so I would have to make sure not to spend all my time staring at the basket-dustballs because I would probably also be at risk of getting my skinny legs stuck in something sticky on top of the bookshelf like an old piece of candy melted down into a small pond.

It occurred to me that a spider could also be up there, and it might suddenly appear right in front of me swinging down on a thick rope like Spiderman. So, assuming my legs weren't stuck in candy residue, which would make them snap right off if I tried to escape, I would fly away very quickly before the spider could lasso me with his sticky rope and tie me down in his web.

Upon further reflection, I decided that maybe being a fly, even briefly, would not be such a good idea because if the spider ate me, who would drive Jack home from his appointment? Jack would come out of his meeting and look around for me and I wouldn't be there. He would go outside and search for me near the car, which would be empty. Then what? So instead I had to be content with sitting on my metal folding chair with my legs crossed reading my book and hoping Jack would be coherent enough to not merit a drug test since I wasn't sure he could pass it. Fortunately for him, his bleary eyes, wrinkled clothing and monosyllabic responses never raised a red flag at all in this office.

I couldn't focus on my book, however, so instead I spent my time glancing around the room, surreptitiously observing the other people waiting there. The two people closest to the entrance were a man and woman seated together and leaning into each other talking. Both of them appeared angry, and their anger grew palpable as their hushed discussion became more animated and their bodies gestured jerkily in a co-dependent dance.

Next to them was a lanky teenage boy sitting with his head hung down and his face covered with his hoodie. He remained absolutely motionless, in sharp contrast to the irritation that energized the first couple. He didn't even seem old enough to have a driver's license, so I wondered if he had ridden his bike here or hitched a ride from friends.

Next were two young men who appeared to be college students, and I reasoned that they had probably been arrested for public drunkenness near the campus. Although they both looked slightly ashamed, they mainly looked hopeful, perhaps because they were now eighteen years old and if they were lucky, they would be able to complete this entire process without their parents ever finding out.

The last seated pair included a pregnant teen-age girl and a woman who was probably her mother. Both were staring straight ahead, not talking to each other. The mother pecked on her phone while her daughter absentmindedly picked at her fingernails. They wore sadness like a wool blanket in the summer heat.

Around the corner in the outer hallway stood a larger group of people who were a distinctly rougher bunch that clearly did not feel comfort-able entering the waiting room and sitting on folding chairs with their legs crossed, chatting in low voices. Not only could they not keep still, but they were all smokers so they darted in and out of the front entrance, pulling one cigarette after another out of their crinkled cigarette packs while keeping their ears cocked to hear if their names were called. In this group was an older woman, gaunt and rugged, but when I looked more closely at her, I began to think maybe she was my age. She darted from one person to another, laughing and sharing stories, and I noticed that she enjoyed the rare honor of being the only person in the entire place who could elicit a smile from some of the people standing on the fringes of the hallway.

The cluster of waiting people continued out into the parking lot, where relatives and friends stood around resting against their cars, checking their phones, or sitting inside their vehicles with the engines running. Several cars had children in them, too young for school, spending their afternoons sitting in the backseat of a car in front of the probation office instead of playing in a park. The parents kept the windows rolled up while they sat in the front seat smoking one cigarette after another, while turning around periodically to shout or slap a squirming child.

When Jack started his probation meetings, he was still groggy from his medication and sat by himself pretending to read a book, but by the end of his probation later that summer, he had become one of the outsiders, pacing back and forth just outside the doorway and smoking silently while waiting to hear his name called.

CHAPTER NINE

The Tower

Lesson learned: when a skateboard starts careening down a hill, you can't stop it.

Jack had decided to attend a small college in Ohio, and so during the summer, between his probation meetings and community service, I bought twin bed sheets and desk organizers. I paid an enrollment deposit and Jack picked out his dorm. I watched Jack take his medicine and swallow it down with a big smile on his face. Later I found out he spit his pills in the trash can. Despite this, he seemed to be doing OK.

We arrived at his college in the last week of August to get him settled into his dorm room. Although I had nagging fears lurking in the corners of my brain, Jack seemed excited to begin his first semester away from home. The late summer temperatures were still a bit high, but I could see how the beautiful campus would be resplendent with fall foliage in a little over a month.

The college was small, with less than 2,000 students, and located on top of the hill of a small town in the middle of Ohio. It was beautiful, with a mixture of Gothic Revival brick and wooden Colonial-style buildings sprinkled about the campus. In the center was a rectangular quad surrounded by brick classrooms and administrative buildings, while the library's stone façade rose up above one end of the quad. The other end opened up to a tree-inhabited green that stretched down the hill toward the arts buildings and museum, meeting up with the health center along the way. Next to the quad was the student union and cafeteria, and further up the hill was the sports complex and the rows of dormitories, all brick buildings three or four stories tall, with wide porches along their fronts. The dorms curved around an oval-shaped road that opened up to a discreet row of parking spots, and this is where I pulled in to begin unloading my car.

Jack arrived early because he had been hired as a videographer for the football team that had already begun practice, so the campus was deserted when we arrived and we spent the entire day unpacking, setting up Jack's room in the quiet dorm building and purchasing all the things that didn't fit in our car for the drive up from Oklahoma. I could tell Jack was anxious for me to leave, so we decided not to eat dinner together but instead he went to the cafeteria with the football team while I ate in the neighboring town where I had reserved a hotel room. My plan was to stop by for a quick visit in the morning before beginning my long drive back home.

I walked into my hotel room, but before I could put down the car keys, Jack texted me "I am at the minor emergency clinic, can you meet me here?" I didn't even bother to text him back, but instead I pulled the door shut, went back downstairs, got back into my car, found the clinic name and address on my GPS and drove directly there.

Jack had gone skateboarding after dinner that first evening, and the hill upon which the campus occupied had proven treacherous. It had just finished raining lightly so as he traveled along the damp path and made a turn, his board slipped slightly sideways and out from under him in a patch of mud. He fell onto the blacktop, rolled a bit, and landed on his hands. A woman walking her dog stopped to help Jack up, and seeing the blood flow down his arms, she decided to drive him to the minor emergency clinic in town.

By the time I arrived from my hotel, the x-ray revealed two broken fingers, one on each hand. The doctor put a splint on each finger so that

Jack's hands looked like lobster claws, and in that way we drove back to campus and I dropped him off with a new bottle of Tylenol PM.

When you look back at a series of events, it would seem as if these events flow from one to the next with no beginning and no end, just a long line of actions looped together that cannot be disentangled. However, when I now look back at the series of events that unfolded through that fall semester, I know that Jack's unraveling began with the broken fingers—the broken fingers were the *terminus ante quem* of this slice of the story. I knew it then, too; I felt it with a vague sense of unease but without realizing what to do about it. And so the next morning, I drove back to campus to say goodbye and my exhausted son, who couldn't sleep because of the pain in his hands, gave me a distracted hug before I started my drive home.

The drive home took fourteen hours, which I divided into two days by stopping in the middle of Missouri for one night. During this time, the gentle and persistent ache in Jack's fingers had not stopped. Instead, it prevented him from sleeping at night, and if there was one thing I knew about bipolar disorder, it was that a lack of sleep needed to be treated swiftly and aggressively, which of course was exactly what did not happen. So, instead of sleeping, Jack began his habit of walking the campus at night, determined to use his time wisely by exploring every building, every floor on every building, every room, and every corner in every room, before the rest of the students arrived the following week.

It was during these nighttime walks that Jack discovered the deer that inhabited the campus at night, the deer that remained so still the only thing you could see were their glowing eyeballs hovering about five feet off the ground like a pair of neon marbles floating mid-air. Once he saw the deer eyes, Jack was transfixed, and each night he tried to move closer and closer to these animals until he could see the dark silhouette outline of each deer's body.

He called me on the phone late one evening while standing in front of the deer and whispered in the phone so he wouldn't scare them away. Although it was dark, he could see the pairs of eyes looking at him from various heights, and in that way he began to learn the little deer from the bigger deer, the males from the females, and sometimes he saw so many eyes that he wondered what it would be like to live with the deer as a family member.

He began a habit of creeping slowly toward the deer, taking his time and moving his arms and legs in a slow and graceful way so the deer would not be afraid, dancing an interpretive dance that he thought they might appreciate, thinking that perhaps they might want to learn the dance as well. He would then stop and slowly move even closer to the deer, creeping forward with his hand out, trying to get close enough to touch them.

One night, Jack had spent so long dancing and standing amidst the deer that they must have forgotten he was there because when he reached his hand out, a fawn walked toward him and brushed her fur against his hand. Mixed with fear and curiosity, the fawn realized what she had done, and she planted her feet on the ground and waited, and even though she was shaking, she let him reach out and touch her again.

In this way Jack was formally introduced to each member of the small herd that frequented the campus at night, and he began to wile away the nighttime hours with the deer, sitting against a tree and staring up at the stars while they lingered nearby, testing his reactions to their movements. This became a nightly ritual, and as Jack slept less and less, he spent more and more time with the deer.

———

If a skateboard is positioned at the top of a hill, velocity begins at zero. The skateboard tips off the edge of the hill and starts to pick up speed as it falls downward, accelerating with the earth's gravitation pull at a rate of 9.8 meters per second squared. The skateboard hits the ground. Is the skateboard accident the tipping point in Jack's college career?

———————

During these long nights when Jack stayed awake, he also began to formulate a set of ideas about how the world was coming to an end, and what he could do about it. He knew that only through knowledge could the world be saved, and he, as a college student with special access to a vast collection of books, was well positioned to make this happen. So, with an increased sense of urgency, Jack began to designate a series of secret hiding spots around campus where he could stockpile the books he thought would be useful as the world began to unravel. Jack carefully documented these plans in his journal, and included a list of the books he hid away.

To prepare for the storage of this influx of books, Jack was first able to secure permission from the librarian to use two senior research desks and to reserve two extra shelves that could be locked behind an iron grate where he could keep his books safe. By then he had already accumulated a large number of books that were stacked up in piles in his dorm room, and he quickly filled his two desks and research shelves with more books, at which point he began to search for a few additional storage areas around campus such as beneath the sofa in the student lounge and under piles of leaves behind several of the trees that lined the edge of the wooded area next to his dormitory building. He knew that he needed secure hiding spots because if people caught on to what he was doing, they might try to dissuade him from his plan. In this way, the library was emptied of every book on Freud, every version of the DSM, and every book on sleep patterns and dream theories.

It was during this time that Jack also learned of the existence of the Government Documents Collection on the eighth-floor tower of the main library. The college library is one of the earliest depositories of state documents in the region and it also holds a collection of important federal documents from the Department of Defense that date back to World War II.

These documents held secrets that required his perusal, Jack reasoned, if he was going to have any chance at saving the world, because these documents provided detailed information on various current threats to national security. If he could get his hands on them, he could prevent World War III from occurring.

Jack then decided to befriend Steve Jobs, who

Jack claimed had faked his own death because he wanted out of the rat race and was currently teaching psychology at the college. Jack emailed me a photograph of this professor and a photograph of Steve Jobs so I could see they were the same person. He was furthermore convinced that Steve Jobs' son was a student there as well, and Jack, in his charming way, quickly befriended so-called Steve Jobs's son and shared his plan to save the world.

The boy, whose real name we'll never know, embraced his new alias wholeheartedly and agreed to partake in the big plans Jack had for the two of them. Who wouldn't want to be a part of this college adventure? One night, they went to the library and stayed until closing, hiding behind a bank of desks and waiting until the library emptied out, the lights turned off, the staff departed, and the doors locked.

Then, armed with a wrench and a flashlight, they tried to unscrew the bolts that held the hinges on the locked Government Documents entrance door with the hope that if they could remove the hinges entirely from the metal frame, they would be able to open the door from the opposite side of the lock. However, the door would not budge, so they gave up after removing only two bolts and they returned downstairs to wait out the night, locked inside the library until the staff returned the next morning.

While his friend napped, Jack used the rest of the night to his advantage by gathering as many books as he could find in the open stacks that focused on government policy and cramming them beneath his two study carrels and stacking the rest of them in neat rows along the wall next to his carrel.

The next morning, the library opened to a seismic shift in its library holdings where the entirety of sections J through JK were stripped of all books, including the folios located on the second floor, all of which were placed in open areas surrounding Jack's two carrels. His goal, which was quickly thwarted, was to gradually take these books out of the library, backpack by backpack, and put them in the basement of his dormitory.

As the skateboard falls, it continues to increase in speed, but when will it come to rest? The time it takes to reach its destination can be calculated as time = $\sqrt{(2y/g)}$. So, if the skateboard falls 200 meters, $t=\sqrt{(2 \times 200)/9.8 \text{ m/s2}}$, it will hit the ground in 6.39 seconds.

The next morning, despite the library fiasco that was explained away as a late-night prank, Jack went to class so as not to create suspicion about his precarious state of mind. However, on that same day he began to notice that someone was shadowing him, following him to each class and sitting next to him during each lecture. He called me at home that afternoon and angrily asked if I knew about this. I told him he must be mistaken and he should get some sleep.

Jack seemed to have slept better that night, because when I called him the next morning he sounded much calmer. He had already gone to his first class and didn't notice anyone following him, and assured me that he felt fine but that he would take an afternoon nap to make certain.

However, just after lunch something very unusual happened on campus—someone called in a bomb threat and the campus went on lockdown for the next two hours. Both campus security and city police swarmed the area and closed off all access to the campus, including the main entrance and all exit routes, while all classes were cancelled and students were required to shelter in their dorms. Men with rifles scoured the area, walking back and forth across the now empty campus patrolling the area while students peeked out of their dorm room windows, waiting for something to happen. For a person teetering on mania, this was one of the worst things that could happen.

During this time, I received an automated message that the school was on lockdown. I knew Jack would be worried, so I called and called and called him, but his phone was dead. At the same time, I kept refreshing the college home page, waiting for an update on the lockdown message.

By 5 p.m. the threat was revealed to be a hoax and the lockdown was lifted. Three high school students had called several other schools with the same threat, and they were promptly arrested while the relieved college students poured outside into the late afternoon sun to enjoy what remained of the beautiful fall day. I continued to call Jack, but I was unable to get through on his phone, which now went straight to voice mail.

Later I learned that Jack did not think this was a simple prank but that it was meant as a distraction while a more comprehensive bombing campaign was being staged at college campuses across the country. So, while all the students were relaxing, Jack was trying to figure out a way to get President Obama to come to campus in order to warn him. Maybe if Jack had a car he would have jumped into it and driven to Washington D.C., but since he didn't, he instead decided that he needed to host the part of the century before World War III began. It was the third weekend of the semester, and he had just learned that the resident advisor would be out of town that weekend.

If Jack starts to fall off his skateboard, he is already

experiencing forward motion even before sliding into the mud. The mud causes his skateboard to decelerate rapidly, which is what makes him fall, and as he falls, his arms fly away from his body and his feet slip out from under his legs, which creates drag and resistance, but these are too many variables for me to calculate. However, I can safely say that he hit the ground in less than 6.39 seconds, which is not nearly enough time for me to catch him.

———————

And so it was, after Jack had fallen off his skateboard, broken his fingers, stopped sleeping because of the ache in his hands, discovered the deer, broken into the Government Documents Collection with Steve Jobs's son, weathered a bomb threat, invited President Obama to campus, spent nine hundred dollars in 45 minutes and hosted the party of the century that he was sent to Rose Hill Behavioral Health Hospital.

That is when I flew up to Ohio, when Jack was released from Rose Hill and given a second chance at college. I drove him back to campus armed with a two-week prescription for aripiprazole. I had a bad feeling about leaving town, however, so I decided to drive back to the dingy hotel I had previously checked out of, and check back in so I could stay around campus a few extra days and see how things were going.

Jack was back at school getting caught up on his classwork and everything could have worked out that way, but unbeknownst to me, he was also not taking his medicine. On the third day I was there, I was sitting on a bench in front of the student union in the middle of the campus enjoying the sunshine and the gentle rhythm of classes beginning and ending with students moving from one building to the next and faculty members walking up and down the quad. I saw Jack round the corner of the classroom building in the distance and he was half walking and half running across the quad toward the student union. I stood up to say hello as he passed me by, but he didn't seem to notice I was there.

After he passed the student union, an elderly woman who I had observed lingering in the quad nearby came up to me and pulled a small statuette of the Indian god Ganesh out of her pocket and handed it to me.

"Your son asked me for this last night," she said, "but he left before I could give it to him."

"I think he will need it," she continued, staring at me.

I looked at it carefully, turning it around in my hands and rubbing the smooth green soapstone between my fingers. Ganesh was seated cross-legged with his big elephant head resting on his chubby neck while his trunk hung over his fleshy, round belly. Four arms reached out from his body, with one hand holding an ax used to cut off worldly attachments and a second hand holding a conch shell. When I was little we learned that if you put your ear to the opening of a conch shell and listen very carefully, you could hear the roar of the ocean. Ganesh tells us that with the conch shell, you can hear your inner voice, your conscience. The third hand was holding a mace that brings us closer to the truth, and the fourth hand was in a gesture of blessing in order to encourage fearless interaction on this earth.

I looked at the figure again, slipped it into my pocket, and thanked her. She nodded her head and turned to walk across the quad toward the parking lot.

This time period was the brief interlude, the intermission, between Jack's first and second hospital stays while in college, a time when I was busy trying to ignore the little whining voice in the back of my head called the "voice of reason." I was busy ignoring this voice so I could enjoy the delusion I had created for myself that told me Jack would recover sufficiently enough to be able to stay in school.

CHAPTER TEN

The Fool

We are playing a zero-sum game; we are in Nash equilibrium. We are math equations waiting for quantification. If, for example, we calculate human emotions on a scale of one to ten with psychopathy resting at 1 and manic-depression at 10, I rate a 6.34. With Omega-3, I can rate a 5.1. If I swim underwater, I can rate a 3.2. Admittedly, I can only swim underwater a short amount of time, so the final calculation must be plus or minus .4. If Jack would take his prescription, he would be a 7.1. But he skips his medicine because he is an escape artist, a rebellious free spirit, so he is a 10.

———————

I spent five days shadowing Jack around campus trying to assess his state-of-mind, all the while thinking about the workshop I had been required to attend concerning the negative impact of "helicopter parenting" on today's children. I am the helicopter parent *par excellence*, running interference between Jack and the world, protecting him from the world, protecting the world from him.

So there I was sitting in the student union, trying to keep a low profile while waiting for Jack to get out of class so I could see if he had slept the night before, if he had changed his clothes, and if he had eaten breakfast—all the things he doesn't do when things go south. The problem, however, was that he was getting good at telling me what I wanted to hear, so I had to get even better at telling the difference. While Jack was in class that week I wandered around the small downtown, walking up and down Main Street browsing through book stores and antique shops, eating lunch at the cute restaurants, and studying the beautiful colonial-style wooden homes with white columned porches and neat gardens. I imagined living there, where things would be so much easier, I thought to myself.

By the end of the week I had developed a full-blown fantasy of how I could rent a *pied-à-terre* somewhere in town and work at the local library. In reality, though, there was nothing more I could do on campus, so I flew back home and went back to work, all the while hoping for the best outcome.

This delusion of mine, the delusion that everything would be OK, lasted two weeks until Jack's college counselor called me one evening to tell me Jack was back in the hospital. This time the message was matter-of-fact, a foregone conclusion, and this time I didn't panic because the ambulance had already transported Jack to the hospital. Since I had missed so much work from the previous trip, I decided I would fly back up to Ohio on the day of his release, which would probably be in five days, I calculated.

Later that first night, however, I was awoken at 1:20 a.m. by several frantic phone calls and a string of text messages from some of Jack's friends. They were all wondering why and how Jack was sending out pictures of himself strapped to a hospital bed with the hashtag #Dreamfreeor-die. Jack had been sent to the same emergency room as before, when he was taken to Rose Hill and given the bottle of little blue pills that remained unopened in the top drawer of his dorm room desk. The nurse even remembered him from before, but this time, instead of immediately tranquilizing him and sending him to Rose Hill to wake up disoriented two days later, they kept him medicine-free so he could be assessed by a different doctor, a doctor who might be able to gain fresh insight into Jack's condition.

Jack was pleased because he figured that would allow him access to yet another person

in the medical industry with whom to com-
miserate about the corrupt state of affairs in the
psychiatric industry. But the doctor was busy and
Jack was wide-awake, so Jack lay in the hospital
bed wearing a light yellow gown with a subtle
floral pattern while propped up against two pillows eyeballing his phone as he scrolled madly
through his Facebook messages. It was one a.m.
when Jack was suddenly struck with an idea, so
he sprang out of bed, yanked out his IV, and ran
out of the room. He had grown bored of lying
in bed waiting for his fate to be determined by
a doctor, so he decided to run off and seek his
own fortune.

Jack ran down the hall as fast as he could,
crossed the reception area and headed toward
the double-door entrance, from where he burst
out of the hospital and into the moonlight:

> *Hickory dickory dock,*
> *The mouse ran up the clock.*
> *The clock struck one,*
> *The mouse ran down,*
> *Hickory dickory dock.*

(attrib. Mother Goose, origin and date unknown)

Once outside, Jack galloped down the sidewalk
barefooted in his loose-fitting hospital gown that
flapped happily in the breeze while the string

ties lining the back loosened themselves and opened up as he ran along. Two police officers were stationed at the hospital that night, but they had been relaxing with the mistaken notion that Jack, who was not given a tranquilizer, would be resting peacefully, willingly, in his hospital room. Instead, the night nurse had to alert them to Jack's escape and they ran out the door after him. The years of swimming and dry land workouts gave Jack an advantage, however, together with the fact that he wasn't weighed down by clothing and shoes. Jack's head start therefore allowed him time to stage an impromptu photo shoot by snapping pictures with his phone all along his escape route.

His photo documentation began with a series of blurry photographs taken at the nurse's station, where two nurses were seated behind the reception desk talking. The women's expressions began to change as they watched Jack running through the foyer.

The photographs, which Jack later posted online, unfolded as a modern *tableau vivant* with these unwitting actors appearing in the first image talking together in hushed tones during what would have been an uneventful night in the hospital of this quiet town. The nurses are turned toward each other, one talking while the other leaning in to listen with her head cocked slightly to the side.

The next image, taken a second later and at a different angle, shows the nurses with two different reactions, much like the spectators depicted in the sacred paintings of the Catholic Reformation. In these religious paintings the viewer invariably sees one witness gazing down at her fingernails while the other witness stares, wide-eyed, at the figure of Christ streaking past them barefooted with his white robe flapping in the breeze, off to spread the news of eternal glory. In this second photograph, the nurse on the left is still talking, still telling her story in her quiet voice, while the nurse on the right, who had been leaning forward to listen, now has turned her head in the other direction to see Jack running past. Her face is frozen in a startled gaze, while her mouth is permanently formed into the shape of an o.

A third photograph, taken further away from the desk when Jack was turning toward the exit, shows both women staring at Jack. The nurse on the left is not telling her story anymore, but instead she braces her hands on the desk while the other nurse is rising up out of her seat with her mouth open, speaking and pointing to someone outside the picture frame while she waves a blurry arm above her head.

The next photograph, shot outside the building, shows a hazy assortment of people, some standing by themselves while others are clustered in small groups. These people left the visitor's room to go outside to stretch, smoke, and talk while waiting and wondering, and in these photographs each person stares blankly with sleep-deprived eyes at Jack while he ran past them snapping photographs along the way. By this time, however, the two police officers were closing in on Jack, and as they ran to catch up to him, he continued to shoot photographs at increasingly odd angles, swinging his phone back and forth without stopping to focus.

The final image is back in focus. Here Jack stopped running and turned, paused, and snapped a single, half-length portrait of one of the police officers right before the officer threw Jack to the ground and handcuffed him.

This image is the most arresting photograph from the series, and not in just a *double entendre* way, but as a study in contrasts, where all movement suddenly stopped and the police officer appeared standing in front of the brick wall of the hospital illuminated by a bright fluorescent streetlight above him. He looks directly out of the photograph at Jack in the moment suspended in time right before he lunged toward Jack. However, instead of bracing himself for the imminent capture of his semi-clad soon-to-be prisoner, the police officer has a tired look on his face and his head is tilted very slightly to the right as if he is asking why. Why? He looks like he would rather be home sleeping soundly than running through the streets in the middle of the night wrestling a wild college student to the ground.

There were two more photographs from that day that Jack took in the afternoon before he was hospitalized. One of them shows Jack's school counselor looking at him with a furrowed brow above a face that appears slightly angry, perhaps, but mainly sad and frustrated. Her face is surrounded by wavy brown hair and she looks upward—she must have been seated as Jack stood before her snapping a photograph, in fact, she probably just sat down at her desk to pick up her phone and dial the number of the ambulance.

The next photograph from that afternoon was a self-portrait taken by Jack during the wild ambulance ride to the emergency room. This image shows Jack lying down on the gurney in his seersucker suit and yellow bowtie and he is lifting his head up to the camera while laughing laughing laughing. This snapshot shows the pure, unadulterated manic joy of the court jester.

After Jack's hospital escape, the police officers escorted him back to his hospital room, where he was tied to his bed and a guard was stationed outside his room. Now he needed to be treated not just for psychosis, but also for road rash since his body had skidded across the concrete. His phone, which was miraculously unharmed during the sidewalk altercation, was placed on the wheeled table positioned across his bed, not completely out of reach. Therefore, he was able to wrestle one arm free from its bed restraint, liberate the other hand, and reach his phone to take one final selfie. In this image, Jack is sitting up in bed, now with a serious look on his face. He holds one hand up, palm facing away, to show his index finger attached to a monitor and a black triangle surrounded by small black circles drawn in the center of his hand with a Sharpie pen. This image is the one sent out with the hashtag #Dreamfreeordie.

It was from his hospital bed that this photo-montage was sent out on Instagram to all of his friends, and it was precisely at 1:20 a.m. that I began to receive phone calls from people, both far and near, who had just witnessed the beginning of Jack's emerging internet notoriety.

———————

The next morning, while Jack was being transported to the State Hospital an hour away in Columbus, I gathered together all the phone numbers I needed to begin my search for people I could talk to about Jack, all the while I hoped he would sign a privacy waiver allowing me to speak with his treatment team. Later that day, I found out that he would be staying at the hospital only a few days, as he would have to get far worse before he could stay longer. When

Jack first arrived, he was on his best behavior, hoping to garner a quick release by proving that nothing was wrong. Fortunately the doctors had seen through this tactic and signed the pink slip, at which point Jack became irate and started to berate his treatment team and complain about their lack of training.

After a day of this, the medicine started to kick in and Jack, now with time to ponder his next course of action, began to wonder if there might be some merit to his diagnosis, to the medications; perhaps some bit of the doctor's information might be correct?

However, just as Jack started to mull over this possibility, the pink slip was up and it was time to leave. This was when Jack started to backpedal, arguing that everything had been a big mistake and nothing was wrong with him. Armed with a new bottle of pills he knew he would never take and a hand full of pamphlets he would never read, he was allowed to leave.

Once I found out about his early release, I rushed to change my plane ticket while trying to extract a promise from Jack's doctor not to release him until I could get there. I had called the night nurse the evening before just to check on Jack and that is when I found out they decided to release him a day early, before I had planned to be there. That would have meant Jack would have been allowed to wander off, down the sidewalk and out into the street with no money, no way home, to disappear into the city. With my hands shaking, I held the phone to my ear and knelt down on the floor of my living room and begged the nurse, as one mother begs another mother, to keep Jack safe until I got there. She listened to me.

So I flew back to the same airport as before and selected a similar rental car, and this time I drove directly to the State Hospital in Columbus, which was much larger and more urban than Rose Hill, but the context was the same, the function was the same. I turned onto the campus and steered my car along the road, following the signs to the visitors' entrance and past the admissions building, where a lone police car sat waiting for something to happen.

Once inside the visitor's entrance, I showed my identification and asked to see Jack. Permission was granted, and I emptied my pockets and left all my possessions in a locker, for which I was given a small key. I was allowed to carry the key with me inside the hospital—it was the key that tethered me to the outside world, separating me from the keyless people locked inside.

I passed through another set of doors into the inner sanctum, where I found one long, wide hallway with a series of smaller hallways branching off at 90% angles, numbered consecutively from 1 to 10. I made a mental note to ask Jack if the psychopaths were all housed along Hallway One, based on my numbering system.

About halfway down the long hallway I passed a man walking back and forth and back and forth, carefully counting ten steps each way while staring at the floor, not even glancing up as I walked by. Obsessive-compulsive disorders must lie in the middle of the spectrum, I thought to myself, on Hallway Five. My mental illness numbering system was obviously correct, as Jack's ward was down Hallway 10.

This ward, which was mercifully designated for younger adults, was arranged like a college dormitory from 1962. It had a tall round reception desk in front of the entrance, a hallway branching off to the right and one off to the left that were both lined with bedrooms, and a commons area on the other side of the desk that was surrounded by small meeting rooms and offices, all with glass walls. The commons area was furnished with chunky wooden crate-style chairs and coffee tables while a nubby burnt orange sofa was placed directly in front of a large television set that was blasting a mindless conversation at top volume to a man lying on the sofa fast asleep. Another young man paced back and forth behind the couch agitatedly screaming, "You stole my thousand dollars, YOU did," and jabbing his finger at nobody in particular.

Jack was happy to see me, his accomplice, and

gave me a tight hug. We sat down at one of the tables and tried to talk, but the noise emanating from the television dominated every inch of the commons area with the sound of newscasters posturing and tattling in their self-important manner, distracting Jack from our conversation. He kept looking up at the television with increased agitation until a news clip came on that featured the drought that was continuing in the southwest and into California, where firefighters were struggling to contain a number of wild fires fueled by the Santa Ana winds.

"See, I told you the world will end in fire; the end is near!" Jack turned to me and proclaimed triumphantly, happy to be correct in his fore-telling of future events.

Jack is the prophet, the new-age Nostrada-mus. Never mind that Yosemite is always on fire. In the coming days, the television would meet the same fate as the telephone had in the previous hospital—it would be ripped off the wall and smashed to pieces, and I was glad of that. Every bit of news about fire, war, or famine only confirmed to Jack that he had been correct about the beginning of World War III.

Then Jack leaned in close to me and I could hear him say gravely "Mom, you have to get me out of here." He nodded his head toward the young man who had been yelling about his money and who was now peering through the glass window into the nurse's office where the nurse was seated at her desk typing on her computer trying to avoid his angry gaze. The young man looked to be about 21 years old and was wearing baggy shorts that, because he was required to be beltless, were hanging down past his knees, a huge white T-shirt and a stiff ball cap resting delicately on the top of his head with the price tag flapping around his ear. He then hunched down to the nurse's level and banged his fist on the window, but the nurse continued to type without even a slight flinch.

"He's my roommate and he whispers in his sleep that he's going to kill me," Jack explained.

"Are there guards stationed outside your door?" I asked.

"They're down the hall," he said. "Mom, I need to get out of here, this place is terrifying."

I sat back in my chair thinking about Jack's safety. Do they really mix violent and non-violent patients in this place? Maybe after this angry outburst the nurse will give Jack's roommate an extra stiff cocktail of meds at dinnertime that would keep him sleeping through the night. I looked across the room at him, but by now he had wandered off and the nurse continued her work without having looked up once.

Across the foyer was a hallway that led down to the men's dorm rooms, and Jack's bedroom was located down there. I wondered what his room looked like. Across the reception area was the girls' hallway, which appeared to be similar. I was thankful that although this hospital was for adults, they kept the younger patients in a separate ward, though I don't know why I was glad about that since perhaps older patients are safer.

Next to the reception desk was a large bulletin board covered in Plexiglas that announced a schedule of activities—art in Hallway 2 on Tuesdays and Thursdays at 10 a.m., jewelry-making on Thursdays at 2 p.m., therapeutic drumming every Wednesday at 3 p.m. in Hallway 4, and interpretive dance every morning in the foyer of Ward 5 after breakfast. Art, not science, is for the inmates, poetry yes, math no, too logical. I hoped Jack had attended some of these sessions.

I looked at Jack, not sure what to do about the roommate situation. Aside from being overdressed for the occasion, Jack appeared healthy, although somewhat pale, but he did not look like he could defend himself. His sleeves were folded up neatly and on one wrist I saw a bracelet he had made in the jewelry class. It had brightly colored beads strung together with letters that spelled the words "sail the mind."

He also wore a yellow rubber bracelet that someone had given him with the word COURAGE written on it in capital letters. I stared at this simple bracelet, this round piece of rubber that was a token gift from a stranger in a hospital

930 miles away from home—and it made me cry. Here was a person taking care of my son and telling him to be courageous, telling him to be courageous in a place where I could not be.

On his other wrist was a third bracelet, another beaded one from the jewelry class, and on this one Jack had strung together four large beads that spelled the letters AWOL. Those four letters signified the definitive end of his first semester at college.

CHAPTER ELEVEN

The Magician

On the Global Assessment Scale, which rates the severity of mental illness on a scale of 0-100, Jack is a 25, which doesn't seem too bad except for the fact that the level of severity goes from 100 downwards, so 25 reveals an inability to function in all areas—work, school, relations with friends and family, and with a serious mood impairment, combative behavior, self-harm, hallucinations or delusions. Therefore, he was admitted to the state hospital with what was described as a grossly impaired ability to recognize reality, and he was released three days later with a one-word notation of condition at discharge: improved.

After Jack was released, he and I returned to campus and packed up all his belongings, signed all the paperwork for a medical withdrawal, and drove fourteen hours back to Oklahoma.

We had been home several weeks and were sitting on the bar stools at the kitchen counter eating grilled cheese sandwiches one day. Jack grabbed a knife to cut one of the sandwiches in half, then he drained his milk in one gulp before slamming it down on the countertop, which made the glass clatter and bump into the change bowl that he had just finished sifting through looking for enough money to buy cigarettes.

Just then, the house phone rang and although I usually don't answer my landline, the number registered from Ohio, so I picked up the receiver and said hello. On the other end was a woman from Community Ambulance Services, and she asked to speak to Jack. I glanced over to see him devouring his sandwich in one bite, and told the woman he wasn't home. She explained that she had tried to contact Jack on several occasions to pay his outstanding ambulance bill, which was 800 dollars, but he had not sent in payment yet and the bill was past due.

I looked back over at Jack and laughed at the thought of him in possession of 800 dollars. An image popped into my mind of him hunched over his desk, carefully tearing a check out of his non-existent checkbook trying not to rip the edges, and then meticulously writing out the sum of money on the correct line, signing the check in cursive and sealing it in an envelope, to be licked and stamped before sending it to the address confirmed with a quick phone call.

"What are you laughing about?" he asked,

and I hoped his voice wasn't loud enough for the woman on the other end of the phone to hear. I didn't answer, nor did he look up at me as I continued to talk on the phone; instead he reached across the table for a second sandwich and dragged it through a pool of ranch dressing on the way to his mouth.

"But we never received a bill from you," I responded into the phone after this brief pause.

"Well, I sent him a phone message about the bill because we didn't have his address," the woman replied.

"You have my address, though, right?" I asked, trying to be helpful. "And you do remember that you drove him to the state mental hospital?" I added. I wondered if perhaps she wasn't aware of where they took Jack, so I held back from trying to give her some advice on how to extract a large sum of money from a person just recovering from psychosis. She didn't answer my question, but instead explained, "Well, HIPAA laws prevent me from talking with you about this, I was just hoping to track him down to pay his bill."

"He doesn't pay his bills, I do," I responded, "so if you want the bill paid, you will have to send it to me." The woman sourly explained that Jack was eighteen years old, not a minor anymore, and although he might have signed off on the release of his medical information at the hospital, the ambulance company had no record of any release form signed by him for their services, so she would have to send the bill to a collection agency if he didn't pay.

I laughed bitterly, "Well go right ahead, then, I don't give a crap!" and hung up. With this last exchange I had Jack's full attention as he turned his head toward me and started to laugh. "You tell those solicitors a thing or two!" he said gleefully.

After the phone conversation, I sat back down next to Jack and waited for him to finish chewing before asking him what he planned to do next. Taking another large bite of sandwich, he stood up from the chair and tightened the belt of his long terrycloth bathrobe. Then he reached down and grabbed a chopstick that was left on the table from his late-night sushi with remnants of sticky rice clinging to the wood. He pointing it high up into the air and announced dramatically, "I am going to build the dream machine!" Rice flew off the stick and landed on the floor.

"How are you going to build it?" I asked.

"I can't explain it to you because it is far too complicated for this conversation," he replied, to which I countered, "I have all day, so why don't we talk about it?"

Jack turned his head up into the air and laughed at me. "I have an entire team of people working with me called the Dreamteam, so if you don't believe me, just wait a few years and you will see."

"What if these friends of yours have other things they want to do?" I reasoned, to which he snorted, "Everyone wants to be involved in my project. What else is there to do?"

"Well, most of your friends are now in college," I responded, "and they're busy with their classes."

Jack pretended not to hear my hurtful comment and went on, explaining to me that unlike the virtual reality devices now on the market, his machine could be manipulated by thought waves alone.

"You mean like a Ouija board?" I said with a laugh.

"Furthermore," he continued, talking over my comment, "these thought waves will eventually be able to be analyzed in such a way that they can be recreated for every type of human experience in existence."

One month ago, Jack had argued that at some point in the near future, once all human emotions are successfully created and catalogued for use on a computer database, we would be able to leave our bodies and enter the dream world permanently, all the while being attached to a computer. According to him, this computerized brain would allow us to extend our lives without the physical constraints and logistical difficulties of the material world, and in this way, we would become immortal.

Meanwhile I worried about what would happen if the woman made good on her promise to send the bill to a collection agency, but my fear was short-lived because two days later I received the bill in the mail, with my full name and complete address carefully written out by hand neatly on the envelope.

———————

When Shiva tells Parvati the world is merely an illusion and that matter doesn't exist, Parvati becomes angry. Parvati is, after all, the mother of the physical world, manifested through her love and devotion; she is the daughter of the king of the Himalayas; she is the soul of the mountains. If the world is just an illusion, Parvati says to Shiva, then you don't need me, and so she leaves the world behind. Because of her disappearance, the sun stops warming the earth, the rain does not fall, and food does not grow. The world is in chaos, which causes much suffering. It is this suffering that proves the world is not an illusion because illusions cannot cause the kind of physical pain that comes from being in the material world.

But Shiva does not want to understand this. He wants to roam, naked and with matted hair, through the universe with no earthly attachments. He dances wildly, like an unpredictable madman, and his violent dancing shatters the cosmos. Shiva loves Parvati but he does not feel the need to demonstrate his love to her, although he tries to show love to his two children, Kartikeya, the strong, athletic boy who became the god of war, and poor little Ganesh, the quiet boy who became the god of intellectual pursuits. Sometimes Shiva acts rashly, however, and puts his children's lives at risk. One day, for example, Shiva mistook Ganesh for an intruder and accidentally cut his head off, but after seeing Parvati stricken with grief and crying, Shiva fashioned Ganesh a new head made from that of an elephant.

On this particular day, while we sat in the kitchen together, Jack fell short of defending his previous hope for a post-human immaterial existence but instead he focused on some of the technological advances in virtual reality and reality enhancement devices that have come onto the market these days. I wondered if his perspective really was shifting, or if he was just getting better at knowing what he could and could not say. If he received external confirmation of his ideas, then did that mean he was in touch with reality or did it just mean he had found enough people willing to agree with him, willing to go on a ride with him? Was his medicine starting to work? I wondered.

He saw that I looked dubious.

"You just think I'm delusional," he said, with a hint of anger in his voice. "A delusion is an incorrect understanding of reality, but who determines what is considered a "correct" version of reality?" he continued in a teacher tone. Clearly he had been reading about psychosis online. "How about I determine that for myself? After all, I am the Magician, you know," he added, smiling, taunting.

I didn't even know how to respond to him because I didn't want to tell Jack that I agreed with some of the things he says but not with everything.

So we sat in silence for a few moments. "Mom, will you read my tarot cards?" he then asked, with a softer voice. "Just like you used to?"

"Honey, that was just a game we played," I sighed.

"You always thought it was real, that is what you told me!" he responded, with his voice projecting at a higher tone.

"OK, OK, I'll get my cards."

I didn't want an argument, so I walked into my bedroom and found my deck of cards with an old rubber band disintegrating around it. I looked through the deck to see if any of the cards were missing, but it was still only the Sun card gone, which was Jack's birth card that I had pulled out of the deck many years ago and tucked into the corner of my bureau. The image of the chubby baby looked just like Jack as a child. The card was still there, held in place between the mirror and its wood frame, so I tugged the card out and placed it back in the deck and returned to the kitchen.

Next I took all the books off the kitchen table, removed the bowl of fruit and the napkins, and I wiped the table clean and took a towel to dry it off completely before setting the cards on its surface. Jack tapped his foot impatiently. Then I started to sort all the cards into their categories—all the trump cards first, beginning with The Fool, which is number zero. "Yes, zero is a number," I whispered to myself. Jack was still seated at the counter watching me, trying to be patient. His leg twitched.

"Look, see how the Fool steps off the precipice," I said, showing him the card.

"He's going on a journey," Jack responded, a correction, while pointing to the hobo sack the Fool was carrying on his shoulder. "The flower in his hand signifies that he is carefree and happy, right?" Jack asked, adding playfully, "He even takes his dog with him!" while pointing at our dog currently lying on the carpet next to the sliding glass door.

For a moment I was reminded of the long drive back to Oklahoma from Boston when I had no food and I had to feed our dog the beef jerky I bought at gas stations along the way, the only places open on Christmas day. I stared at the picture of the Fool standing next to his dog, which I had never noticed before looked like a little white terrier, our dog.

I picked up the next card. "The Magician comes next, trying to fix things, I guess," I said, showing Jack the second trump card, thinking that was perhaps the card that referred to me. Jack nodded thoughtfully, clearly feeling a sense of confirmation in the proclamation he had just made a few minutes ago about himself being a magician.

I counted through the rest of the cards, stopping to glance at the Wheel of Fortune before sorting all the way to the last card, the World, at number 21. Next I separated out the cups, pentacles, wands, and swords, counting through the ten cards for each set plus the four face cards for each, totaling 14 cards x 4 suits + 21 trumps = 77. I could tell that Jack was growing impatient, so I shuffled the cards several times and asked him to cut the deck three times while I went to the living room to find my tarot reference book, which I figured I would need since I hadn't studied my cards in several years.

I returned to the kitchen with the dog-eared paperback, sat down and shuffled the cards three more times before laying them out in a Celtic spread, the only pattern I had ever used. A present situation card, a crossing card, one card above, one card below, one card behind, one card in front. The next four cards I placed to the right of the cross, going from top to bottom, so that a total of ten cards were resting face up on the table, some right side up, some upside down. Seeing the cards ready, Jack shifted down from the counter barstool to a chair at the table next to me.

"What is my birth card again?" he asked, glancing at the cards.

"Oh, it's the Sun," I said. "I just made that up a long time ago, however."

Jack frowned. "But you told me you had your cards read when I was a baby, and that was my card!"

He was correct, I did have my cards read, I thought to myself, by an old woman I met at a Renaissance festival. She was a fortuneteller, but while the other fortunetellers were wearing costumes, she sat inside her tent all alone and reminded me of my grandmother, sitting there and smiling to herself. I peered in the tent to ask if she did readings, and she nodded yes, but explained that it was too late to do my reading that day, but she invited me out to her house for a reading the next day. I had just moved to Oklahoma and I was lonely and needed someone to talk to, so I said yes.

The next day I drove out to the trailer park where the woman lived out in the country forty minutes away from my home. She opened the screen door and I stepped up the cinderblocks into her kitchen and sat at her kitchen table while she cleared off her books, wiped down the table, and dried it with a towel before spreading her worn cards into a pattern I had never seen before, the Celtic cross. Before starting the reading, she pressed a button on an old cassette player located at the edge of the table so she could record a tape for me to take home, which I no longer have.

The reading frightened me, and I got the sense that the fortuneteller was leaving out some important information. After she finished, I thanked her and took my tape home, and the next day I bought a tarot deck for myself. A week later I took the Sun card out of the deck and tucked it into the mirror of my bedroom bureau, returning it to the deck every time I did a reading.

Although the Sun card was the centerpiece of the reading the woman gave me that day, another card figured prominently in the card spread that I had never told anyone about. It was the card of Temperance, which I didn't know how to interpret at the time. Indeed, the woman had trouble interpreting the card too, I remember that, and she said something about not telling the truth, or perhaps a car accident and the police helping, but it seemed that people were helping me, so she said I shouldn't worry. I didn't worry, until now, that is, some eighteen years later.

Jack leaned across me to get a better look at the

Celtic cross spread I just laid out. He immediately noticed the upside down card of Temperance in the crossing position, and he looked up at me and grinned like the Cheshire cat. My heart sank.

Later that evening I was sorting through the clothing that remained in Jack's luggage from college. When we returned home a few weeks ago, Jack dumped everything in his closet unopened and I was just beginning to sort through his things and wash his clothing with the hope he would start wearing something besides the terrycloth bathrobe that had not left his body since he arrived home.

Inside one suitcase I found a black plastic trash bag—it was one of the garbage bags we had hastily stuffed with his clothing and bedding in his dorm room the day he withdrew from college. The bag was damp, and when I opened it the smell of mildew and vodka issued forth from several towels that were mixed in with the clothing. I pulled the towels out and put them aside to bleach, and then I sorted through the rest of the clothing, checking all the pockets before dumping the load into the washing machine. In one pocket I found the small, green soapstone carving of Ganesh with his giant elephant head that the elderly campus woman had given Jack. I wondered how this little statue was ever going to protect him.

CHAPTER TWELVE

The Star and
the Aqueous Angel

Jack had the habit of taking long walks at night, sometimes for one or two hours at a time to calm his brain and slow down the chatter of his thoughts. One fall evening he seemed extra agitated, so I decided to sleep in the living room so I would wake up if he left the house, and I could see where he was going from the big picture window. A left turn meant he was going down to his friend's house; a right turn took him to the neighborhood park. I dragged two pillows and two blankets to the couch, and eventually fell asleep fitfully, dreaming in fragments.

This particular night was a beautiful, star-filled autumn night, perfect for an evening somnambulation, and so Jack slipped out the front door without even waking me from my restless couch sleep. He cut across the front yard, turned right, and started to walk down the middle of the empty street, pausing once to light a cigarette beneath the streetlight before heading two streets away to the park where he usually roamed after dark.

A creek ran through the center of the park, which was lined with trees, a narrow path on one side, and a playground and open field on the other side. He walked along the creek on the narrow side where the dirt path was well worn, then he turned right to follow the curve of the creek and walked toward a cluster of trees that stood across from the deserted playground. As he walked along, he tried not to trip over the shallow tree roots that jutted out of the ground while he was gazing up at the twisted silhouettes of these Oklahoma trees that live a life of drought in the summer and ice storms in the winter.

It was now early November and the warm weather had given over to a cool, pleasant temperature with a slight dampness in the night air. Jack followed the path through the park and out the other side, but his thoughts were still racing in his head so he decided to turn left instead of right, and take a longer walk than usual, this time through town.

He found a sidewalk that continued through the neighborhood on the other side of the park from our house, and walked past the houses into town, where he started to see the shuttered shop fronts and dark library and closed office buildings, and he kept walking all the way down Main Street, through town to the other side, where houses began again. He walked through those neighborhoods until the yards grew bigger and the houses got farther and farther apart until the sidewalks ended and the houses disappeared altogether.

He kept walking until the roads turned into dirt paths and the flat land began to grow into gentle hills. He didn't remember ever seeing these hills from town, but that didn't seem strange to him because he was preoccupied with his internal dialogue that didn't quiet down with the walk but instead grew louder and louder until he began to feel what seemed like an electric current run through his entire body that at first felt like a fever but then it tingled like when you are hit with an adrenaline rush, but, instead of fading away, the tingling sensation grew stronger and stronger as it seemed to course through both his veins and his muscles, sending spasms into his chest.

It was then that he noticed a young woman who appeared out of nowhere standing at the edge of a shallow pool of water. The air around her seemed electric, and the water sparkled and glittered as she knelt down in front of it and began to dip water into an earthenware pitcher.

She turned and poured the water onto the ground next to the pool, and then she dipped the pitcher back into the water and poured it out again, repeating this action over and over. Jack watched this process and grew more and more curious, so he stepped out of the shadows where he had been lurking and walked toward the woman.

"Why are you pouring water into the ground?" he asked.

"I must water the earth so the trees will grow and the soil will come back to life," she responded, smiling.

Jack then saw that the woman was naked, which, oddly enough, he had not noticed until now, but it didn't seem strange to him at all. The woman's body shimmered and her hair sparkled as if she had stepped directly out of the water so as to rejuvenate the earth with her own corporeal presence.

Suddenly Jack realized how thirsty he was, so he bent down to the ground, cupped his hands together, and began to drink heartily from the pool of water. He drank and drank and drank. But when he stood back up, the woman was gone. This, too, did not seem odd to him.

He shifted his attention to the stars above his head, which gradually appeared closer and closer to him the more he stared upward. In fact, they seemed so close that he thought he could reach out and touch them, but when he stretched his arms up above his head, the stars slipped back up into the night sky, away in the distance, leaving his grasping hands, fingers pointed upward.

———————

Before the universe there was nothing, in the same way that before we are born, we do not exist, unless we existed in another time and place, the same of which can be said for the universe. At one moment and for reasons unknown, gravitational pressure became so intense that it compressed matter into density, and space-time was born out of dark energy.

As the clock of time started to tick-tock, the primordial soup of our universe splattered outward, with matter and anti-matter colliding and creating energy until matter won out, and so our carnal existence was preordained. The soup cooled rapidly and the ingredients began to mingle and emerge, one proton and one electron, and then two protons and two electrons, hydrogen and helium.

———————

One is hydrogen, two is helium, and three is lithium—the three primal elements that were created in the first three minutes of the birth of the universe.

Once gravity collapsed, the solar nebula began to spin in upon itself like a raw egg poaching in swirling water, and chunks of matter solidified to create the sun, the moon, and the planets. The elements that formed the earth collided and compressed with this continual spinning until they were bound together into a sphere, while ice chunks and other debris were pulled to the earth's surface by the warp of space-time that causes gravity.

Before, there was nothing. Then there was matter, then water. It was this water that leached lithium from the rocks that came from the solar system onto the earth's crust, three protons, three electrons, four neutrons now coursing through the earth's water streams and soaking into the earth's crust from the pitcher of life, settling into the soil and igneous rocks, *lithos*. Shimmering, silvery white, floating, on fire, turning black, now found in all organisms on earth. Lithium was present at the beginning of time some 13.7 billion years ago, three minutes after the beginning of time to be precise, and now lithium is present in Jack's new medicine, 300 milligrams three times a day.

One is hydrogen, two is helium, and three is lithium—one is movement, two is inertia, three is equilibrium.

After drinking the water, Jack reached up toward the stars, trying to calculate the distance to them from Earth by the measurement of his thumb. He sat down on one of the large rocks surrounding the pool and looked around at the dark landscape that was strangely beautiful in its sparkling quietude. In this moment he started to feel calmer than he had felt in a very long time. The stars twinkled in the sky above him, burning primordial lithium over his head. He stood up and recited aloud:

> *Star light, star bright,*
> *The first star I see tonight,*
> *I wish I may, I wish I might,*
> *Have the wish I wish tonight.*

(English author, date unknown)

Then he turned abruptly and began to walk back home.

Usually, if Jack saw me sleeping on the couch when he went out at night, he would slip back into the house via the back door or through his bedroom window to keep me from knowing he had been gone. This time, however, he entered through the front door, ambling in very calmly and not furtively, and when he saw me on the couch where I had just woken up to the sound of the dog growling, he gave me a warm smile as if his late-night departure was normal and his safe return a foregone conclusion.

"I am feeling so much better now," he said, and he turned down the hall toward his bedroom, clicked off his light, climbed into bed, and promptly fell asleep with a silence of the mind that he hadn't experienced in a long time.

One is heaven, two is the earth, and three is the abyss.

CHAPTER THIRTEEN

Intemperance

A week later, I dreamed of the same woman, kneeling next to the same shimmering pool of water. On this night, however, Jack in my dreams strode through the park and came up to the woman abruptly, knowing she would be there. When she saw him, she stood up startled, and I could see that on this evening she was clothed in a long white dress and had wings that came up from behind her shoulders.

As she rose to a standing position, she stepped away from the pool and began to shift from one foot to the other while pouring water from one ceramic vessel into another, pouring back and forth until the water began to change colors, growing darker and redder, until it turned from water into wine. The woman paused a moment, looked up from her task, and gazed straight into Jack's blue eyes with her beautiful, angelic face. She threw her head back and erupted into peals of laughter.

Jack retreated, not sure of what to do, but as he backed away from the woman he lingered at the water's edge, fascinated by her presence. The woman dipped one foot into the shallow water and dragged her toes around in a slow circle, looking at him intently while flapping her wings ever so slightly, creating a gentle stirring of the air around both of them.

She reached across to him and handed him the pitcher of wine. With a smile on her face, she invited him to drink, and Jack drank and drank but the wine never seemed to disappear, so he kept drinking until the woman snatched the pitcher back from him angrily and smashed it to the ground, where it shattered into a million shimmering pieces.

"You are crossing boundaries that shouldn't be crossed," she hissed.

Jack stumbled toward the woman and stood in front of her, swaying on his feet while his own anger welled up inside of him. "You don't know what you are talking about, I am doing nothing wrong," he argued.

"You must know the meaning of moderation," she replied. "Never drink all the wine, but always leave half of the pitcher full."

"Half full, half empty, who cares! I can drink it all if I want to!" he responded.

The woman shook her head from left to right, "The wine is an illusion. Although you will feel better while you are here in the dreaming, once you wake, you will feel worse."

"I'll stay in the dream world, then," Jack replied.

Again the woman shook her head, this time more slowly from left to right. "You live a carnal existence and must learn to navigate the physical world."

"I don't care about reality if it only includes the things of the waking world," Jack replied.

Jack looked around and refocused his attention on the woman, who stood there before him with her left hand on her hip while her right arm encircled the pitcher that was now back in one piece.

He then began to see her as if he were seeing her for the first time. In front of the woman was the pool of water, still shimmering a deep blue, and behind the woman was a gentle hill rising to her right and a flowery meadow to her left, all bathed in the light of the moon hanging low in the sky. Jack saw a road off in the distance tracking through the hills, and he realized he was tired and wanted to go home. He looked back at the woman and cocked his head slightly.

"Please drive me home now," he said to her with an imperious tone, "I'm really tired."

"Well, I can't, because I don't have a car," she responded impatiently.

Jack puffed out his cheeks and said angrily,

"Never mind, then, I'll walk," and he stormed off toward the distant path.

————————

The next morning Jack awoke in a foul mood and refused to get out of bed until 1 p.m., at which point he ambled into the kitchen wearing the same clothes he had on the previous evening, minus the shoes. His body and clothing emanated the sweet, pungent stink of alcohol mixed with cigarettes covered over by the cloying odor of the incense he liked to burn in his room.

"Are you going to shower?" I asked him.

"Maybe later," he responded, "what's for breakfast?"

I had just finished cooking four eggs and two pieces of toast, which I put down on the table in front of him. He sat down and looked at his food, took two bites, and pushed the plate away. Despite his lack of sleep, Jack was fidgety and looked preoccupied, as if he was entertaining various thoughts simultaneously.

"I've decided to take my medicine only when I want to," he declared.

I put down my coffee and sighed.

He continued, "The doctors don't know what is going on inside my brain—it is my brain, and they can't possibly know unless they go into my brain and get out all my knowledge."

I sighed again. "Do you want to go to the library?" I asked, since I knew there was no winning this argument.

Jack pulled out his phone and scrolled through his messages. Once he confirmed that he had no friend available to better my offer, he agreed, and we spent an hour at the public library where I browsed the shelves to find a mystery book while Jack found a book on how to be a CEO and another book on how to recognize psychopaths. After checking out, we returned to the car and he settled in the back seat. I pulled out of the parking lot and started the drive home as he toyed with his library books absentmindedly.

"I never want to go back to college, you know," he reminded me yet again, and then explained, "I can learn all I need to know on the Internet. I can download syllabi from Harvard University if I want to."

"But how are you going to seek out knowledge on your own about things you don't know exist?" I asked. "How are you going to learn new subjects?"

"I am a genius, and listening to stupid people makes my brain hurt," he spat out, looking up at me with cold eyes. "You just don't understand, you don't open your mind up, other people know what I am talking about," he spoke with an increasingly hostile tone of voice.

Jack was gearing up for a grand soliloquy, and I knew that anything I could say would be talked over, so I fell silent. Now I just wanted the slow traffic to speed up so I could get home as quickly as possible.

"Please please please don't say anything," I whispered to myself.

Jack leaned up toward the front seat, "What did you say?"

"Nothing, I was just talking to myself," I responded.

"You always do that," he laughed bitterly. "And I'm the crazy one."

At that point I turned off my ears so that my heart would not hurt, but Jack fell silent, and when we got back home we walked into the house separately. Jack sprawled on the sofa to scroll through his phone messages while I went to my bedroom and shut the door. Fighting back tears, I crawled into my bed but I was too agitated to stay there, so I got back up and walked around my bedroom in circles.

"I really need to keep my shit together," I said to myself, but, not knowing how to do that, I instead sat back down on my bed, propped the pillows behind me and closed my eyes while trying to calm myself down.

I breathed in deeply, expanding my rib cage with oxygen to calm the beats of my heart into a slow rhythm. I sat there about five minutes, fighting back my urge to check on Jack. Instead I tried to sweep all the words out of my brain and waited for the alpha waves to replace the beta waves through absolute breath control.

I thought of a moving golden line that ropes up and down and gradually flattens out into one straight line until it doesn't appear to move at all. My breathing started to slow down, 18, 17, 16 times a minute to 5, as I exhaled slowly and slowly, counting my breaths.

Next I forced myself to smile, making sure to relax all of the muscles in my forehead. I opened my eyes a bit, which makes a smile appear more genuine. I started to relax and think of myself floating down the street waving at people. What good things do I offer to the world? I began to think of my list of positive traits, all the while strangers were smiling back at me.

Then I imagined my kindness forming like a ball of shimmering invisible thread that slowly unwound and moved away from me to flow toward other people, binding us together as humans who walk this earth and suffer in common.

Finally, I thought of Jack as a little boy, the chubby Sagittarius baby running along the water's edge with his blond wispy hair flapping in the breeze. He turned and turned in circles, laughing a deep and long laugh while looking up at me.

"It's time to go," I said to him, "We need to get back home."

"I'm not leaving," he teased, and just as he

began to run away from me once more, I reached out to catch him, embracing him tightly in my arms while he tried to squirm free.

"You can't make me leave; you're not the boss of me!" he laughed, gleefully stomping his feet.

Then he seemed to have a change of heart. "OK, let's go home now," he said, "so you can read me a book."

I gazed down at Jack, who was still a toddler, and my impatience fell away as time slowed down. I tried to freeze this memory in my mind so that one day in the future, some time in my life, I would be able to recreate this moment and hold my little boy again, hear his high-pitched voice, feel his soft, sticky hands, and taste the salty air on his baby cheeks.

Jack stared back up at me, "When we get home, you will read me a story, right?" he asked, with a look of concern on his face.

"I will always read you a story," I responded.

With the echoes of this memory back in my bedroom, I closed my eyes and imagined the golden thread of loving kindness traveling from me to my grown son. I cast the thread outward toward him in order to hold him with compassion, not anger.

CHAPTER FOURTEEN

The Empress

In May, several months after Jack was born, we moved from Boston to Oklahoma, where I had been hired to work part-time at an art museum. It was now the middle of summer and the heat had settled over the entire town. Our house was a one-story white wood home with a wide porch that stretched across the house and a picket fence that wrapped around the yard from front to back. I had gotten into the habit of rocking my baby, and myself, in a creaky hammock swing until the streets emptied out and the neighborhood became quiet. When I was certain Jack was asleep, I would lay him down on a square pillow wrapped in a sheet and I would settle once again in the swing to sip from a tall glass of iced tea until I got too tired to stay awake.

Each summer morning I woke up early enough to take Jack outside to play while the air was still fresh, and then I would carry

him to his daycare down the street and hand
him over before heading through town to the
museum, where I was still learning the intricacies of my new job. After lunch I would pick
him up from daycare and return home, where
we would escape the heat by staying indoors,
lying on a futon together with a fan blowing
warm air on our feet while we rested. I watched
his miniature fingers flailing in the air while
he slept, waving furiously at nothing. It is not
easy being born, I thought to myself, and I felt
sorry for him.

Baby Jack gradually began to look around his
new world, first squinting at the light fixtures
and then staring into my face. What could he
see? His eyes followed the movement of light,
the shadows, and then they began to focus for
fleeting moments on particular objects. He must
have been nearly blind, I thought, able only to
see dramatic contrasts between light and dark
and the movement of objects within this new,
hazy world. Being born from the darkness into
the light must be shocking.

While I rocked him, his arms would slowly
relax and he would begin to rest his legs on mine
while falling deeper and deeper into sleep. What
was he thinking about? Without words, babies
must dream their hopes of warmth, milk, of floating asleep. While they are sleeping, babies must
also notice how something inside of them beats

rhythmically—tick-tock, but without knowing how to count one two three four five six seven eight nine ten, they don't equate this beating with the passing of time but with a feeling of comfort that flows continuously across time. They must know that the rhythm that comes from inside of them is familiar and consistent with the beating sound that has surrounded them since they first felt their existence. Maybe they recognize that their breath follows a similar rhythm, much like the breathing they feel coming from people around them.

As they begin to perceive these consistent patterns that will form the circadian rhythm of their lives, surely they are comforted by the *normae* and *regulae* of their consciousness. These patterns help babies find a harmony within themselves and the world around them, and slowly they learn to recognize that there is an order to their lives that is the root of their survival.

One night, while sitting on the porch swing, it occurred to me that only when babies realize this do they begin to smile. From darkness into light, from a tiny world into an infinite one, from abstract thought to a world of concrete ideas, this is how things work. On this particular evening it was almost midnight, the last day of July, when Jack finally fell asleep on my lap on the front porch. I gathered him up and started to walk back into the house.

As I walked through the door, I turned to look out into the front yard at the two short, mangled trees that obscured the sky with their jagged branches, both located to the side of the house and creating a stiff silhouette in my peripheral vision. Out in the yard the grass had grown tall and the irises rose up magnificently tangled around the edges of the grass while the roses clung to the side of the fence, twining through the sweet peas.

I gladly sacrificed my sleep at night to experience this solitude, while the cool night air gave temporary relief from the blistering summer heat of the Oklahoma sun. The moon was small that night so the park in front of my house was completely dark and I could only see to the edges of my yard. I turned back into the house, and baby Jack shifted in my arms as I accidentally bumped my tea glass against the metal frame of the door, but he didn't wake up. I eased through the door and carefully shut the screen behind me.

When I first moved to Oklahoma, I noticed how the landscape changed gradually from the picturesque hills and green grass of the East Coast to the richer colors of the south, with its thick vegetation and high humidity. Driving here for the first time, I remember arriving at the top of the last peak of the Ouachita Mountain range that separates Arkansas from Oklahoma, where I was startled to see the vast flat earth suddenly unfold in front of me like a threadbare carpet stretching to infinity. That was Oklahoma—the entire state, lying there in front of me, with no trees to block my view. It seemed as if I could see the whole world all at once. In my childhood dreams of Oklahoma, however, I never really saw what it looked like, I just felt it.

So, I pulled over into a lookout area on top of the mountain and parked my car. I had passed very few vehicles along the way, and nobody else pulled over to this rest stop, so I stood there alone, gasping for air as I stared out across the land. The lookout area was a public works project that dated back to the WPA, and it had a small parking lot with a sidewalk that stretched along the edge of the mountain lined by a rickety bent metal railing that was clearly added as a feeble attempt to restrain any potential fallers or jumpers. Below the railing someone had added chicken wire attached to the posts that stretched across to cover the entire lower portion of the railing, which otherwise would have been wide open to the possibility of a child stepping beneath it and plummeting to a certain death. I held on to the railing but kept my feet back a few inches from the edge because the sidewalk next to the chicken wire had begun to crumble away.

What would Leonardo da Vinci draw from this vantage point? He would probably begin by drawing a line through the middle of a sheet of paper, signaling the separation of sky from land. But when I looked out into the distance, I couldn't see the horizon line, so Leonardo would have to make his pencil line blurry by rubbing it with his fingers. Then, he would have to draw some clouds in the sky so viewers would know what they were looking at, but on that particular day there were no clouds across the dry state of Oklahoma. Instead, the blue sky and brown ground mingled together so everything looked like a swirling brown–blue mixture. If Leonardo were sketching Oklahoma he could get by with using only two colors—a bit of blue mixed into the brown pencil and blended with his fingertips.

I looked again across the landscape, and since this part of the state is sparsely inhabited, I couldn't see any houses, roads, rivers, or anything else that might draw my eye across the land into the distance. So, Leonardo might need to add some buildings for scale, or perhaps a path or a river winding through the land to show how it stretched off into the distance, all imagined using his sense of *invenzione*.

I looked up into the sky where the sun glinted downward and dispersed its rays across the land, revealing a hot, hazy atmosphere. This space between objects was exactly what had fascinated Leonardo da Vinci, who liked to create a *sfumato,* a smoky haziness in his drawings that in this sketch would have to consume the entire sheet of paper. The final sketch of Oklahoma, then, would reveal nothing but emptiness to one person, but another person might see the entire universe in his drawing.

I got back into my car and continued driving, down the mountain and across the flat landscape until I arrived at the town where my new job was located. This town has a beautiful, empty Main Street with shop front remnants of an earlier era located north of a bustling university campus. The surrounding frame houses of the historical downtown built in the heyday of the 1920s are a mixture of quaint shabbiness and upscale renovations. Meanwhile, the town has been expanding rapidly around its outskirts with the addition of hundreds of housing developments and subdivisions, strip malls and fast food restaurants, all lined up along a straight path of fat highway that slices the town into two parts, east and west.

One cool evening shortly after I had arrived in Oklahoma, I was driving around this downtown trying to get my son to fall asleep in his car seat, and I came across a small house listed for sale with a homemade sign posted in the front yard.

I pulled up in front of the house and saw an old man who appeared to be in his eighties, standing on a ladder furiously scraping paint chips off the wooden slats of the exterior in preparation for a new coat of creamy white paint.

I called up to him and offered to buy the house right then and there, and although he first gave me a strange look, he quickly sized me up and agreed that the house would suit me perfectly. He climbed down the ladder and offered to show me the inside, which he had just painted a uniform light jade green.

As he showed me the two small bedrooms and bathroom, he explained to me that after he retired he had started to buy old houses to renovate, giving them, one by one, to each of his granddaughters. He had many granddaughters so he bought many houses, and this task had taken him twenty years.

Now, although he had no houseless-granddaughters left, he continued to buy houses and renovate them, not knowing what else to do with his time. This was the first house he had put on the market to sell. And since I reminded him of one of his granddaughters, he agreed to sell me the house without any bank references. The next day he finished painting the exterior, and the following week I signed the loan papers and moved in with my infant son, one futon, two suitcases of clothing, and several boxes of books. On the following Sunday, I read the man's obituary in the local newspaper.

———————

The years tumbled by and Jack grew into a round, towheaded boy who loved school and playing make-believe in the park. One day, when he was eight years old, he came running down the street breathless. This was the first year I let him walk home from school alone, now that he was in third grade, but he wasn't really alone because two other children also walked the same route, starting from behind the elementary school and cutting through the park before walking down the street one block first to our house, then around the corner to their two houses.

Jack ran ahead of his two friends, going as fast as he could. I had arranged my work schedule so I could always be home when school let out, and I would stand in the kitchen and watch the clock until the time when the school bell would ring, then I would wait five more minutes before walking out the front door and crossing the lawn diagonally until I could see down the street where Jack would soon turn the corner and run toward me, usually laughing, unless he was crying. I always asked him if he looked both ways before crossing the street and he replied "most of the time." I would give him a worried look, and he would laugh.

"Today I finished writing my poem!" he exclaimed, and thrust a piece of paper in my hand. I read it:

I am dull and gloomy.
I wonder if I have a psychic gift.
I hear a waterfall.
I see the future.
I want peace.
I am dull and gloomy.

I pretend to fly.
I feel the wind.
I touch the clouds.
I worry about life.
I cry about death.
I am dull and gloomy.

(Mrs. Schlueter's class, Lincoln Elementary)

"This poem is beautiful," I started off. Then I bent down closer to his face so I could ask, "But are you sad?"

"Of course not, silly!" he responded, looking up into my eyes and cocking his head slightly. "I wanted to make it sound dramatic and show a lot of emotion. That is what we were supposed to do!"

"OK, good," I said, feeling relieved. "It is a

beautiful poem, very emotional." Then I changed the subject, "Do you remember what we are going to do today?"

He looked around the front yard, "Sure, where is the tree?"

I pointed to a small plant five feet tall and very thin. Jack frowned, clearly he had hoped for a larger tree, but that was all I could afford.

"It's small now, but it will grow quickly," I explained.

He continued to look at the tree. "Will you be dead before it gets tall?" he asked, now looking worried.

"Of course not! It will grow tall the same way you will grow tall, and when you are a grown-up, it will be grown up too!"

I gave him my best smile and handed him a small shovel. We spent the next hour selecting a spot for the tree in our front yard and digging a large hole, which was exhausting because red Oklahoma dirt is hard to dig into, so we filled the hole with buckets of water and continued to dig, filling it with water, and then digging again until we had a hole deep enough for the tree roots.

We lowered the tree into the hole and I covered the roots with mud while Jack held the thin trunk in place with his short arms. It was an early spring day so the grass was already green and the tree had small buds on it, ready to bloom. Once we had the mud packed down, we stood back from our work to make sure the tree was straight, then we walked around the tree trunk pressing the dirt down with our feet. Finally, we took the garden hose and watered the area thoroughly.

The tree grew quickly, each year becoming taller and thicker, and within the next five years the tree had gone from the skinny branch we had to brace against the wind to a tree as tall as our house that shaded our entire front yard and killed off the grass, which I tried unsuccessfully to replace each year. During this time, Jack moved on from elementary school to middle school, taking the bus to and from sixth grade with an ever-growing group of neighborhood kids.

Jack grew taller, his feet larger and his legs longer. He learned to ride a skateboard and he grew his hair long, which he trained to curve to the side and around his face. He began to like girls, but he was too goofy to be taken seriously. Instead, he filled our home with his neighborhood friends so that each day, when I came home from work, I would find the house overflowing with kids working on film projects or making comedy shows, writing music, or reciting poetry. Sometimes the furniture in my entire house would be moved around to create a stage set, other times my closets would be raided for costumes. It was during this time I bought Jack his first video camera and he began to film movies throughout the house and out into the streets of our neighborhood.

Jack learned to edit his films, and with these skills my house became magical, where black holes suddenly appeared in the kitchen floor and the living room carpet burst into flames. A bowl on my dining room table featured dancing fruit, while my bedroom had floating furniture. One time our neighbor's house exploded. Another time the street in front of our house ruptured open, creating a large hole from which people emerged wearing long black robes. The creek in our neighborhood park turned into the River Styx and Jack rode by on a horse, wearing a red cape. Eventually, Jack learned to fly, to fly high up into the sky, which was a precursor to his teen years.

CHAPTER FIFTEEN

The Chariot

It was when Jack was in eighth grade that I received my first middle-of-the-night phone call, the type of phone call every parent fears. Jack had three friends spending the night that evening, and although I tried to stay up until they fell asleep, they kept playing video games on and on, going back and forth into the kitchen to grab more chips, more soda, until I could not raise my head up from my pillow.

When the call came on my house phone, I was too sleepy to be afraid so I lay in bed and didn't answer because I was half asleep and half awake dreaming that a random telemarketer from another time zone was calling me about a new roof and that made me angry, but then I thought perhaps a creature from another planet was trying to crack open a portal of communication to talk with a human from the earthly realm—that being me—but this creature clearly didn't know that humans sleep during these dark hours when electromagnetic radiation waves best penetrate the earth's atmosphere. I pondered this thought in my sleep and decided it was too risky to attempt communication with an alien who might want to kidnap me. The phone stopped ringing, and at that point I woke up a bit more because I heard someone leaving a message on my answering machine at 3 a.m., and it sounded like a human being.

I flew out of bed and ran to the kitchen, but by the time I got there and lifted the receiver of my house phone, the caller had finished leaving a message and hung up. I pressed the voicemail button on my answering machine and listened.

"Good Morning! This is Juvenile Services, and we have your son." The woman gave his full name so I would know the message was not an error, but I still doubted her. Before calling back, I put down the phone and ran down the hall to Jack's bedroom, where I slowly opened the door, carefully sneaked in, and peered through the darkness to find two of his friends asleep on the carpeted floor while nobody was in the bunk beds. There, instead of the forms of two more bodies covered by blankets, I saw two blankets lying crumpled on the mattresses next to two pillows, each with the indent of a prior head pressed into the soft feathers. I counted two boys there and two boys gone, which meant that another parent just received the same phone call as me while the other two parents remained fast asleep as their boys were resting easy on the floor of my house.

I ran back to the kitchen and pressed the voicemail button again so I could hear the entire message. The woman left a phone number that I called, and when she answered, she began talking easy and assured me that Jack was OK, he was there and I could come pick him up.

I drove across the sleepy town passing only two cars along the way and pulled into the parking lot of a small gray building used for the sole purpose of diverting minors from the jail downtown so parents could pick their kids up from here, in friendlier surroundings, where they enjoyed a slight bit of temporary protection and comfort only offered to those younger than eighteen. Jack was fourteen.

I exited my car and walked across the parking lot, passing a police officer returning to her car located next to mine. "Are you one of the parents?" she asked, trying to hold back a laugh.

"Yes," I responded a bit distractedly, not thinking about her laughter until I turned to walk through the door and spotted Jack seated in the waiting area with a grim look on his face and dressed as Frodo Baggins. Next to Jack sat the friend whose head had made the indentation on the second feather pillow back at my house, and in his hands was a huge Mexican sombrero, the kind you throw down on the ground and cheerfully dance around ta-da, da da da, ta-da da da. But he, too, was staring straight ahead, and both of them refused to look at me when I walked into the room. I heard another car pull into the parking lot, and then the boy's father arrived. We looked at each other smiling sheepishly, both in our hastily thrown-on clothing like it was just another day in the neighborhood.

After the paperwork was processed, I took Jack home and he went straight to his bedroom without saying a word and promptly fell asleep on the floor next to his two other friends, who had never woken up at all. I stood on the back porch and cried a little bit, then I sneaked back into Jack's bedroom to observe the boys sleeping soundly, and with the apprehension gone from Jack's face, I could see the remnants of his little-boy features.

By the next morning, when the sun began to hit the window and the light started to rouse them from their slumber, the boys awoke knowing this day would require some explanations. And so Jack's friends, hoping to beat a hasty retreat from my house before the questions started, called their parents from the bedroom to request rides home, and then they gathered their belongings and stood on the front porch waiting to be picked up, hoping they could slip away unseen without breakfast.

What had happened that night? Jack and his friends planned to film a movie, but once they escaped through the bathroom window with cameras and costumes they realized the screenplay was not written, and so they wandered up and down the streets at 2 a.m. wondering what comes next. What does come next in this situation? What comes next is a sixteen-year old girl with a newly issued driver's license, that is what.

So, this girl, the cousin of one of the friends, eased her father's white Jeep Cherokee out of the family garage and drove across town at 2:10 a.m. to rescue her younger cousin and his friends from boredom, and the boys rejoiced in their lucky golden chariot ride. All four boys piled into the car and the girl drove around the neighborhood while they discussed what to do, now five teenagers in a car driving around in circles at 2:20 a.m.

They decided to film themselves, so the girl pulled over and Jack and one friend got out of the car, but then the girl drove off laughing, a fun prank as long as nobody falls under the wheels of the car, and she headed back to my house and dropped the two remaining boys off, where they sneaked back through the bathroom window and promptly fell asleep on the floor of my son's bedroom. Meanwhile, Jack and his other friend started to walk home until they were spotted by a police officer. The officer stopped and asked the boys for an explanation of their late night stroll, of which they had none.

When Jack woke up the next morning, he found a notebook and began to think of a title for the book he decided to write about the unlawful and unruly misbehavior that would soon define his teenage years. My son tried to make light of this particular situation by reasoning that, since the police officer knew it would be difficult to film a movie in the dark and when you don't have a plot, she helped them shape a storyline by handcuffing them and driving them in her police car to the juvenile center where they were charged with violating the city curfew ordinance. She was the officer who was laughing while leaving the Juvenile Services building as I arrived that night.

Two months later, we stood outside the courtroom waiting to see the judge. Jack was wearing tan khakis and a nice collared shirt while I hovered behind him hoping he'd say the right things. After the hearing was over, I stood with the parents of the other boy and while we tried to make small talk, we laughed a bit and said to each other, "If this is as bad as things get, I guess we are lucky!"

A few years later, my son got his driver's license and began to drive himself to school in the morning and then to swim practice in the afternoon. He had signed up for several AP classes and joined numerous clubs at his high school, overcommitting himself to the point where he was always busy trying to complete his work, maintain a 4.0 GPA, garner high scores on his standardized tests, make movies, and write poetry. I was worried that he always seemed frantic, but I was proud that he was so involved at school.

One day, I recounted to my friend what I thought was a funny story, but my friend didn't laugh when I told her the events of that day. I initially found it amusing that Jack had driven to my place of work in his underwear, and when my friend looked at me with big, hesitating eyes, I tried to explain it away by saying "...but he didn't even get out of the car." Only then did I begin to wonder if her worried assessment of the situation was more correct than mine.

The morning that happened, I had decided to walk to work, and I left the house just as Jack was rolling out of bed to get ready for school, but by the end of the day I was too tired to walk home, so I called him to pick me up from the museum. He had just returned home from after-school swim practice, so he answered his phone quickly and agreed to come get me, glad for any excuse to get behind the wheel of his car. Jack was a junior in high school and we could never have imagined that his driver's license—that very important piece of laminated plastic signaling freedom and adulthood—would remain in his possession only six more months before being reclaimed by the State of Oklahoma via a letter he received in the mail from the Department of Motor Vehicles.

So on this day I waited in my office finishing up some emails while listening for the phone call that would tell me he was waiting downstairs. A few moments later, my phone rang and when I answered I heard Jack on the other end whispering loudly, "Hurry up Mom, people are starting to look at me like I am weird!" I quickly gathered my books and headed down the stairs and outside the building, thinking that he was worried about having to park illegally in front of the museum.

I then saw Jack sitting in the car in front of the main entrance, hunkered down with both hands on the steering wheel looking around nervously at the people walking past the car in both directions, all of whom seemed oblivious to his shirtless presence inside the vehicle. As I got closer to the car, however, I realized that he was also not wearing any pants, just his boxers, no socks, no shoes, no wallet, no driver's license. He was too busy looking around to see me, so it startled him when I opened the door and got in the passenger's seat.

"Why aren't you dressed?" I asked, and he jerked his head around to stare at me as if my question was impertinent.

"I just got back from swim practice and was taking a shower, so I didn't have time to get dressed!" he responded with a sense of desperation in his voice. "You needed a ride home, and I have a million things to do today!" I suddenly felt sorry that I had asked him for a ride when he was so busy, and I thanked him for coming to pick me up and quickly shut the door so we could get back home.

With that he pressed his toes down into the gas pedal and the engine roared as we hurtled toward home faster than the speed limited allowed. I gripped the door handle, "Please slow down, you're going to get another speeding ticket!" He looked at me and laughed, "I've only gotten one ticket and you always tell me to slow down! I won't get another ticket!"

"How do you know that?" I tested him. "Because I won't," he responded as if the issue was now settled. Two red lights gratefully slowed his progress as he drummed his fingers impatiently on the steering wheel and grabbed his phone to check his texts.

"Put your phone down!" I exclaimed as the light turned green and the car surged forward again before turning right and mercifully slowing down over the speed bumps into our neighborhood. Jack swung his car into the driveway, narrowly missing my car, clicked off the engine, and yanked the keys out of the ignition.

He then jumped out of the car, ducked under the garage door that was still traveling up on its tracks, and disappeared into the house.

I grabbed my books from the back seat and followed him inside, where I saw across the living room that Jack's bedroom door was already shut behind him. He must have sprinted through the house, as light shined from beneath the door and I could hear the sounds of music playing on his computer.

I went to the kitchen and began to sort through my mail when I heard a knock at the front door. My friend, who lives a few doors down from me, had seen us return home and decided to stop by to say hello before starting her daily three-mile run. It was a warm March evening that was beginning to show the signs of spring, so we went to the back patio to enjoy the remaining sunlight. I could hear Jack's stereo at a high volume and the heavy beats of his music followed us outside.

While we were talking, the sun went behind the clouds and the temperature dropped a few degrees. As the shadows grew longer across the concrete, my friend and I decided to split a beer. After that, we each drank another beer, and she then decided she wouldn't go on a run after all. I felt guilty that I had derailed her plans—if she hadn't stopped by to say hello, she would just now be rounding the corner toward my house with a thin layer of sweat on her face, breathing slowly but deeply as she quickened her pace for the final sprint to her house. I would watch her from my kitchen window, running past my house as I rinsed the dishes and cleared off the counter to begin preparing dinner. I always felt a pang of guilt watching her run by, wishing that I was out running too, remembering when I was a few pounds lighter and could run a 5K in under 25 minutes.

My friend sat there looking at me with her brow furrowed. It was getting slightly chilly outside, but I hoped she might stay a bit longer.

"I guess I thought it was funny," I said, trying to sort through the day's events after I told her about Jack driving to pick me up from work in his underwear.

"I mean, it wasn't 'normal,' but nothing Jack does it normal, right? In his realm of normal, I would say this fits in," I tried to explain.

"What is that supposed to mean?" my friend responded, looking at me from the top of her beer.

"Well, remember when he first joined the swim team and I had to buy him that tiny speedo with the high school logo squeezed onto the side of the suit? He didn't even want to put it on, but then remember how he got used to it by wearing it around the house?" My friend nodded, wondering where I was going with this discussion.

When he first began to wear that swimsuit,

he was too embarrassed to walk around in it and always tied a towel around his waist because he felt naked. Then one day I looked out the window to see him standing in the middle of our front yard, wearing nothing but that speedo while talking to the girl who lives two doors down from us. When the conversation ended, he came back in the house laughing. He had slipped his cell phone underneath the side of his speedo and the thin scrap of fabric was straining to hold the phone in place against his pelvic bone.

After that, Jack began to wear his swimsuit with more confidence. When the high school swimmers forgot to bring their running shorts and shoes for their weekly dry land workouts, the coach required them to run through town in their swimsuits, so Jack began to purposefully leave his running gear at home so that he could experience this unique opportunity of running through town barely clad, joyful yet in total accordance with the law.

"You know, Mom," he said to me at the time, "I can wear my speedo in public and it's totally legal, but if I wear my boxer shorts, I'm breaking the law even though my boxer shorts cover more of my legs!"

My friend then said, "So now he thinks he can drive around town in his boxer shorts?"

"I don't know, I think he's just testing boundaries, like teenagers do?" I responded with a statement that ended in a question. It was clearly more than that, I thought to myself as I drained the rest of my beer, but I couldn't put the pieces of the puzzle together.

"Do you want another beer?" I asked my friend as she finished hers at the same time as me.

"No, I need to get home, I think my husband will be back soon and we are going to watch a movie," she responded, standing up and stretching as she transitioned from sitting to moving toward the door.

After she left, I pulled another beer out of the refrigerator and went back to the patio. It was starting to get dark but I continued to sit outside, thinking about Jack and his car. When he first got his license, he rejoiced in this new freedom and drove himself to school and to the swimming pool every day, so I didn't have to worry about dropping him off and picking him up anymore.

Things seemed fine for a while, but then Jack always seemed to be anxious about something. One day he was late for swim practice and got pulled over driving 100 miles an hour down a residential street. Another day Jack dented his tire rims while flying over a speed bump at top speed. His car, an old hatchback, gradually became covered with more and more scratches and scrapes, and Jack frequently returned home with mud splattered up the sides of the car and caked in the wheel wells. Where was he driving? He would never tell me, so I searched the car for clues.

The interior of the car didn't give me any information, however, it just became increasingly filthier and filthier. I found Styrofoam cups with bits of sticky liquid in the back seat of the car, lighters in the seat pockets, remnants of junk food and trash on the floor. There were sheets and blankets in the trunk of the car, in addition to piles of school books left there through the entire spring semester until enough rain had seeped into the hatchback to dampen everything, making the pages of the books curl around their edges and grow mildew in their bindings. The entire car smelled like old cigarette smoke and mold.

One day, Jack drove home with the side mirror smashed, which he claimed happened when he was parked at school, and another time the entire hood of the car was covered with a thick light brown liquid, which Jack identified as a mocha chip latte that his friend poured onto his car during an argument.

I just looked at him and asked the open-ended question of "why?" to which he responded, laughing, "Don't worry Mom, it was happy hour at Starbucks!"

Another time Jack was driving behind his friend's car, following him to a restaurant after swim practice, when he slammed into the back of the car, crushing his friend's bumper. After this, I became more and more worried about Jack, so one morning I decided to follow him in my car on his way to school. I pulled out behind him, as I often do, but then I noticed that instead of turning right down Boyd Street toward the high school, he turned left. I turned left too, and he didn't seem to notice, so I followed behind him for a few blocks and then I drove up next to him at a red light. I looked across at him, willing him to see me, but he just stared straight ahead with his entire torso thumping up and down to his music. He turned left at the light, which took him further away from the high school, and since I couldn't be late for work, I turned right toward the museum.

Later that evening I asked him where he had been going, and he explained that he was just picking up a book at a friend's house, which only made him a few minutes late for school. I wanted to believe him, so I did. Later I found out that during school hours Jack would go over to a friend's house, wait until his parents left for work, and then he would climb into his friend's bedroom window and fall asleep, utterly exhausted after having stayed up all night.

The majority of Jack's mental decline took place that year, and although he tried to disguise it and he refused to talk to me about it, either by lying or by hiding in his room, he could not hide his car. His car was his instability made tangible.

CHAPTER SIXTEEN

The Lovers
(in the past position)

I stood far back from the street because in Rome the cars sometimes turn right up and over the curb to park on the sidewalk, even at the bus stop where I was standing. The bus that I took to my university classes every day usually arrived a few minutes after some driver had just abandoned his car half on the sidewalk and half in the bus lane, and so the bus driver would barrel into the stop while pressing down on his horn and cursing out the window, jamming the bus at a diagonal right up behind the car, blocking two narrow lanes of traffic behind him.

On this particular day, the bus driver's horn was accompanied by the horns of all the cars now blocked in behind the bus, which created a symphony of noise that made my head ache. The noise was loud enough that it forced the car driver to leave his place in line at the pharmacy and sprint back across traffic to move his car out of the way while the bus driver waited impatiently and the cars behind him escalated the angry claxon cacophony until finally the car was gone and the bus driver swooped into the now open spot and jerked the doors open to simultaneously disgorge and retrieve passengers.

I looked at my watch, hoping that this worse-than usual traffic along the bus route would not make me late for my exam. I fought my way onto the bus and clung to the sticky metal pole that is supposed to help keep people standing upright during the ride, and in that way I swayed back and forth as the bus swung along through the traffic, stopping abruptly here and there to deliver passengers along the way. The Gianicolense route was always crowded and I was never lucky enough to have a seat on the bus, so I strapped my backpack to my front to protect it from pickpockets and braced myself as the bus lurched right and then began its slow descent down the long hill toward Trastevere.

I craned my neck to see out the window because once we crossed the bridge, I would sometimes get out and walk the rest of the way so I could stretch my legs and escape the throngs of people pressing up against me on the bus, but today I worried that walking would make me late for my exam, so I held my breath and stayed on the bus until I got to my stop. The bus never slowed down, so once I started to see the street open up to the Roman ruins in Largo di Torre Argentina, I started to push my way forward toward the door, pressing against people who were also lined up to exit, all of us shouting "permesso!" with a grim smile on our faces while waiting for our chance to lunge forward and out of the bus the moment the doors folded open.

I had come to Rome two months ago, in January, to spend the spring semester of my junior year of college studying art history abroad, but although I had been going to college in Boston, I was still not used to the noise, the crowds, and the constant chaos of city life in Italy. Today, since I had an exam, I wore a pretty red sweater and a short black skirt with heels. I dressed well with the hope that my professor would appreciate my efforts to look good, and I carried the textbook he wrote, hoping it would be noticed during the test. After the exam, I planned to meet my friend in Piazza Navona. Spring was right around the corner and I could feel the energy of the city that would soon be transformed into a tourist destination for the next several months.

I had met my friend when I first arrived in Rome; she lived in my same apartment building and I watched her exercise in the garden below while I practiced my Italian above so that I could talk to her. Every morning I stood on the balcony, six stories up, watching this black-haired girl with glasses run back and forth, around the shrubbery and across the patio, circling around and around, and then doing leg lifts and arm swirls for about twenty minutes. She was very thin and I worried she might lose more weight while exercising, so I was glad to see her exercise program was not too rigorous.

One morning I came out into the garden with my running shoes on and she laughed and motioned me to join her. She and I immediately became friends. Each morning we ran circles around the garden while the elderly woman who lived on the first floor snickered at our attempts to avoid bumping into each other. Eventually, when I wanted to go for a proper run down the street, my friend taught me a few nasty things to say to the boys who made comments along the way.

Rome is dark and cold in the winter, but now that the days were longer, I began to look forward to our late-night dinners and wild drives around the city on her Vespa. It was still chilly in the evenings, however, and the wind whipping around us as we drove along at maximum velocity made us feel like we would freeze to death. Unlike in the United States, however, even on the coldest days we were never alone because the sidewalks were always filled with people dressed in their long sweaters, wool pants and fur coats, walking and talking their way across the city.

My friend was studying at the University of Rome and she always seemed to be surrounded by stacks of books so that days would go by and I wouldn't see her, but then she would suddenly call me to ask if I wanted to meet her somewhere. On this particular day, we had arranged to meet in Piazza Navona after our exams and hang out, waiting for something fun to happen.

After my exam was over, I exited the auditorium and immediately saw her in the swarm of students walking out of the building, so I pushed my way forward to catch up with her, and together we crossed the street and walked along the narrow sidewalk to the fountain at Piazza Navona. Along the way we stopped at McDonald's, which was across from the Pantheon, and we bought a fried cherry pie to share. Although I could eat a whole one myself, we always shared one so my friend would not get sick eating American fast food, while I couldn't complain because it was McDonald's and I was in Rome, need I say more?

I was standing there eating my part of the pie when a male student jogged up to me in the piazza and bowed deeply while crossing his arms on his chest, and then he rose back up to look into my face. He adjusted his thick black glasses and looked at me again, staring at my face for a reaction. I started to laugh when I recognized him from my exam, and he laughed too. The exams were always held in that big auditorium, with several taking place at the same time, so there were hundreds of students milling about waiting their turn, joking and laughing.

Despite the crowds, this particular student had stood out to me because while we were waiting he made a clown of himself imitating the dialect and mannerisms of one of our professors, and although I was afraid the teacher would see him, he didn't seem to care. Then, when it was his turn for the oral portion of the exam, I stood back and watched him adjust his glasses, step up, and answer all the questions quickly, correctly, and with a cocky sense of ease, gesturing along with his answers as if he had rehearsed his poses in advance. Later I learned that although he was widely considered one of the smartest students at the university, nobody knew anything about him and he didn't appear to have any friends.

So when I started laughing at him in the piazza, a laugh delayed from his pre-exam antics, he started laughing too, and he introduced himself with an accent I couldn't place. He was thin, with a wiry build, taller than me, and he had a head of thick, brown, unruly hair that swirled across his forehead. He wore a white shirt, rumpled black pants with an elastic waistband and elastic bottoms, and black espadrilles. Meanwhile, my friend just stood there holding her pie while we laughed, and she stared at him with a puzzled look on her face while he ignored her completely.

He seemed to be an odd person, which was interesting, so when he proposed the idea that he and I should meet the next day at the station downtown and take the train to Santa Marinella where we could walk around the beach and have a nice meal together, I agreed. My friend was now looking at me from the side, nudging me that it was time to go. I could tell that she didn't approve of this invitation, so I said goodbye, climbed on my friend's Vespa, and, with me sitting behind holding on to her tightly around her waist, we drove back down the Corso, across the Tiber River, and through the Trastevere neighborhood populated with diners lingering outside the expensive restaurants. We then began the long ride up the Viale di Trastevere to the Gianicolense, and down the street to where we lived twenty minutes from downtown.

The next day, my new friend and I met in front of the train station as planned, and I noticed that he was wearing the same clothing he had on the day before. Once he saw that I actually showed up at our predetermined location on time, his face turned into a big, incredulous smile. It was a bit chillier than the day before had been, so I brought a sweater for the beach and hoped the train would not be too crowded.

We got seats together, and he grabbed my hand and squeezed it happily, like a child, as the train pulled out of the station. We barely talked on the ride to the beach, but I noticed my new friend hummed happily and looking out the window, not bothered at all by our lack of conversation. I wasn't sure what to think.

Once we arrived, we got off the train together and started walking toward the beach. I thought I would begin the conversation, so I asked where he was from and learned that he was from Athens and considered himself a photographer, but he hoped to become a filmmaker, which is why he was in Rome, to study the work of Federico Fellini. He was at the university only to please his parents, he explained, and they wired him money every month if he stayed enrolled in classes, so he was studying linguistics. The exams he took yesterday were merely a charade, he noted, as the majority of his time was spent taking photographs.

"Well, you seemed to do pretty well on those exams, for a charade," I said, "You got the highest score in the class!" to which he laughed. It was then that I noticed the small black bag strapped across his waist, as he reached into it and pulled out a camera and then a lens and attached them together.

And so we walked along the beach, me with my skirt and sandals, and him with his pant legs rolled up and carrying his espadrilles, walking and talking while I collected a few seashells along the way. Finally we arrived at a small restaurant near the walkway, and even though it was slightly chilly, we sat in the patio and had just enough money to split a plate of mussels and a bottle of wine.

The two of us, from different countries, had met in a third country, and so it was that third language we spoke together, neither of us perfectly, but well enough to obscure the social awkwardness that comes with a new friendship. Mundane words and straightforward conversations take on a higher level of interest when you speak them in another language, and so I had finally met someone like me, a person cast adrift far from home.

We continued to talk while the sun went down, the shadows lengthened and the restaurant grew quiet. I began to wonder when the train returned to Rome, and I was just about to ask him when he suddenly jumped up from the table, kicked back his chair, and walked over to a group of older women sitting together on a bench against the restaurant wall. He had been wanting to take their photograph all afternoon and had just that moment gotten up enough courage to ask them, and they laughed a little and asked why, teasing him. He shrugged his shoulders and smiled sheepishly, but then they relented and he circled around them taking more photographs than I thought necessary, so I stood up and came over next to him, and after taking a few more photos, he thanked the women and we walked back to the table where I had asked for the check.

On the train ride home, he seemed energized by our discussion of photography, and he explained the intricacies of outdoor low lighting conditions when taking portraits, and then he showed me a few of the photographs he had taken of the women that were saved on his camera. I looked closely at the first image of the three women together, the beautiful way the figures were carefully cropped. All three women were wearing dark clothing, but one woman had a gold cross around her neck that I hadn't noticed before, and another woman was much younger than the other two. Although I remember the women laughing at the restaurant, when I looked into their faces in the picture, the first woman seemed to be looking straight into the camera with a tight, sad smile while the second woman appeared distracted and the third woman had a slight grimace on her face. The second woman, who was not looking in the camera, had her head turned away slightly, as if she was noticing something behind the right side of my friend's shoulder. Her hands were tensely pressed into her legs, which were crossed at the ankles, while the other two women had their hands loosely folded in their laps. I wondered what the second woman had been looking at so intently, but my friend merely stared at the image with his brow furrowed. I thought it was a beautiful picture.

———————

Spring turned into summer and the temperatures grew warmer and the days longer, and my photographer friend and I were beginning to spend a lot of time together to the point where I started to consider him my boyfriend, my Greek boyfriend in Rome, I, his American girlfriend in Italy. We walked hand-in-hand through the streets of Rome, occasionally gaining stares. By now I had also stopped trying to dress nicely, and I would instead throw on some of his clothing after we woke in the late morning and we would stumble out the door of his apartment building sleepy-eyed and looking for a cup of coffee. Eventually we spent all our time together, and on days when we didn't feel like talking, we would sit together in his sunlit room reading from the stacks of books piled around his floor.

One summer day, I was traveling on the city bus headed to Feltrinelli bookstore in Largo Argentina when I noticed two American boys about my age, glancing at me sideways. They had shiny blond hair, broad shoulders, and they wore college shirts and slouching jeans with a casual ease that the Italian boys sought to emulate with little success. One boy crossed his legs and slipped his hand in his pocket while leaning against the window, and the other boy was turned away from me, swaying around on the heels of his running shoes, trying to balance himself as the bus lurched forward. Both of them laughed. I looked down at their shoes and envisioned how they probably slipped those same feet into ski boots in the winter and strapped them into beach sandals in the summer, and how they probably padded across the wood floors of their big American homes to grab a snack from their kitchen while wearing thick socks scrunched down at the ankles.

I imagined the boys now here in Rome, in the evenings gathered with friends at a bar after just having purchased a nice pair of Italian leather shoes with slight points in the toe. Perhaps they were showing off their shoes while ordering food in English without even trying to speak Italian, and handing over money for the waiter to sort out rather than counting out the correct amount themselves.

At that moment I felt a pain in my gut that I knew was sadness, and I realized it was because I missed the United States. I missed the way Americans open their mouths to laugh loudly, revealing perfect white teeth, I missed the way they shamelessly admitted their errors, without pretense. I missed the carefree way these boys stood on the bus, and I suddenly had the urge to strike up a conversation with them. Up until now I had been acting as if I belonged in the city of Rome, that I blended in, but on this day I wanted to reach out across the row of seats that separated me from them on the bus and to be with this golden-haired pair; I wanted to be the third friend who would return with them to college back at home where we would reminisce about our trip to Rome while drinking beer and laughing at the absurd situations we had found ourselves in.

So I turned toward them and, pushing my hair away from my face, I tilted my head and smiled slowly, with my lips pursed slightly. That was usually all I needed to do to strike up a conversation in Rome. I knew that sometimes the men I flirted with were married, but I didn't care. Sometimes I would pretend to be their wife, or even their daughter, while the men would walk next to me, with chests puffed up like proud peacocks. The two American boys glanced over at me, and then one turned his head as if looking back out the window and they both looked at each other and laughed again. I hesitated a moment before I realized what was happening. Were they mocking me, or was it confusion? I envisioned telling them that I was a college student too and that we probably had a lot of things in common, but they clearly wanted nothing to do with me. Now both turned on their heels, facing away from me, whispering. Stunned, I retreated to a seat in the back of the bus, my eyes stinging with tears.

I caught a glimpse of myself in the glass of the window as I walked to the back seats, and suddenly I realized how much I had changed in the past few months. I was not the girl who had arrived in Rome in January wearing a short skirt and pointy shoes, dragging my suitcase out of the back seat of a taxi as the driver fumbled nervously to help me carry it across the curb while leaning into my arm a bit too closely.

My first night in Rome, I had been filled with excitement and I ventured out on the town all by myself, making friends that first evening. Soon after, I learned the language and the city with relative ease. When I first met my boyfriend, however, we clung together like Siamese twins, and since then, all my other friendships had grown distant. So, here I was on the bus, wearing a dingy shirt that was clearly too big for me, and I hadn't brushed my hair in two days. I had dirt under my fingernails and I tried to remember the last time I had showered, but could not. What was happening to me?

CHAPTER SEVENTEEN

Five of Cups

As the heat of the summer set in, and just when I had become comfortable with the idea of falling in love, I started to notice that my boyfriend was increasingly preoccupied with his own thoughts. First it seemed inconsequential; those nights he wanted to walk home alone, or to not go out with me at all. The quirky, comical behavior that had originally attracted me to him was slowly being replaced with a quiet brooding moodiness that I found equally compelling, but it was precisely during those times he kept me at arm's length. Sometimes he would disappear for days and then reappear as if nothing had happened, and he would look right into my eyes and wrap his arms around my waist, wondering aloud why I seemed so puzzled by his absences.

It was during this same time that he began to complain that his arms itched, and indeed they were rubbed raw from where he scratched them constantly. I bought several different types of lotions that I thought might help, but the bottles remained unopened on his bathroom counter while he continued to complain that perhaps his apartment had bedbugs, although I could find none. Every day he made a trip down to the superintendent's office to ask him to come up and check his apartment, and the repeated visits began to embarrass me. I would smile at the superintendent and shrug my shoulders and roll my eyes, with the gesture of "sorry, what can we do here?"

I found it increasingly difficult to spend time at my boyfriend's apartment since he never sat still but paced back and forth uncomfortably, and as time went on, he began to stare at himself in the mirror, obsessing over his appearance, worried that the itching would spread across his body. At times he would carry on entire gesture-filled conversations in front of the mirror, and the more he spoke to himself, the less he talked to me. I reasoned that he was not like other people, he was an artist, and that is why I found him so interesting.

One evening in the late summer I had gone to the bookstore and it was late when I finished reading so I decided to walk the three miles back home to avoid taking the bus. Walking alone was risky, but I found that if I moved along at a hurried pace and with my head down, I was not harassed and I could get home in less than one hour.

I had just crossed the bridge and turned down Viale Trastevere when I started to regret my decision to walk that long distance with the hill looming in front of me, so I turned in front of the English-language movie theater to take a short-cut down the narrow street next to the theater, and right when I made the turn I looked up to see my boyfriend striding forward toward me, coming from the opposite direction. He was clearly deep in thought, gesturing and talking to himself. I quickly ducked behind a doorway so he wouldn't see me. He passed by me very closely but he was so wrapped up in his own conversation that he didn't notice me peering from around the doorway.

After he walked past me, I stepped out from my hiding place, and feeling confident that he would not turn around to look, I started to follow him. In this way I was able to study his appearance from behind, which I had never had the occasion to do before. I noticed for the first time that he had a very slight limp, when did he start having that? I wondered. It was not actually a limp, I decided after looking again, but he seemed to drag one leg ever so slightly more slowly along the ground before picking it up and placing it in front of the other leg.

It was just a fraction of a second, but as I

studied his gait more closely, I saw how this flickering hesitation in one leg echoed through his
entire body, first with a slight twist of the hips
that had to pause a brief second before helping
to shift weight to the other leg, then the torso
hesitating before following the hips, and finally,
the shoulders, up and down and up and down,
rising and falling gently, slightly out of sync now
with the rest of the body. This resulted in what
seemed like a slight lurch forward with every
step. Indeed, this way of walking didn't seem to
be a new gait, but the familiar movement of a
person who had always moved forward in this
way. How had I not noticed this before?

I continued to follow him, staying half a block
behind and he turned down a narrower street
and then another street until there were no more
pedestrians, no more open doors, no more lights,
no more sounds, and then he stopped, turned to
his right, and deftly lifted the iron latch of an old
wooden door in the center of a plain-looking
stone building. He then swung the door open
and walked into what appeared to be a completely dark room. He reached his hand behind
him to grab the latch and pulled the door shut
so that I could see no more.

I stood there stunned, not knowing what to
do next. I wanted to knock on the door and ask
him why he had just entered a building that was
completely dark and empty, but that would be

ridiculous. However, it would have made more sense to me if I had spotted a person inside, a light on, or heard a sound. I backed up away from the building and looked closely at its exterior. The building was a small three-story structure that appeared to be quite old, with rotted wooden window frames and the outline of an arched doorway, the kind that used to open up to a storefront. Nothing from the exterior explained to me why he would be there. I stood rooted in my spot a few more minutes, thinking he might exit the building soon, but hearing no sound, I decided that all I could do was to continue home and hope for an answer tomorrow. I found my way down the street and turned onto several smaller alleys before seeing a larger street that I recognized, and I followed that street home.

The next morning I woke up early, hot and sticky with sweat after having tossed and turned all night long while dreaming fitfully about abandoned buildings. As I lay in bed wondering about my boyfriend, I decided to get up and walk back to the mysterious house of yesterday, which was a good thirty minutes from my apartment. I started off in the reverse of my direction last night, wondering if I would recognize the house in daylight. After a while I found the alley that linked the small street from the main street I had traveled along, and a few streets later I was pacing back and forth in front of what looked like the same building as last night. I was beginning to doubt myself, however, because this neighborhood was filled with many of these old buildings; some were the back entrances of bakeries, some were woodworking shops, and others were abandoned structures where teenagers gathered when skipping school.

The door through which my boyfriend had entered was still shut, with the latch hanging down. I noticed the latch had no lock on it, which explained the ease in which he had entered the building last night. I then noticed a small window to the upper left of the door that had not appeared to me in the dark of last night, and I could not stop myself from standing on my toes and looking through the window and inside the room. Although it was dark inside, there was enough light to reveal an empty space, devoid of furniture. In the corner I saw a dirty mat on the floor and what appeared to be a pile of towels in the corner.

I began to think of a way to ask my boyfriend about this place the next time I saw him. Unable to contain my curiosity, I decided to walk across the city to his apartment. The walk took an hour, and it gave me the time needed to construct a way I could explain how I saw him last night. As I walked along the streets, the cafes started to open their doors, the metal shuttered gates began to roll up. People were exiting their apartment buildings and filling the sidewalks. A few cars passed by me, then one bus, then another, and finally the traffic picked up to breathe life back into the sleeping city. Surely I had made a mistake about that building, I thought to myself.

By the time I arrived at my boyfriend's apartment, the streets were awake with life and my apprehension was beginning to wane. I became convinced that I had made an error in what I saw last night. I walked up three flights of stairs and knocked on his door, and he opened it immediately, as if he had been standing directly behind the door with his hand on the doorknob. He gave me a slow smile like he had been expecting me and did not seem startled at all to see me standing there. Instead, he slipped his arm around me for a hug while I tried to conceal my shaking hands.

I was determined not to question him and to act like this chance visit was entirely normal. He invited me into his apartment and I quickly looked around. Nothing seemed any different—his futon was on the floor in front of the window with a bedside table rising up next to it. Two bottles of half-empty mineral water were sitting on top of several books resting in cigarette ashes. Opposite the bed was a ripped poster of Che Guevera taped on the wall above a bookcase of concrete blocks alternating between planks of wood that formed shelves. I noticed that most of the books were gone, replaced by several pairs of shoes lined up on the shelves.

Across the room was the table that we had made from a wooden door resting on milk crates and covered by a tablecloth. We had stolen the crates behind the grocery store after they closed and brought them upstairs once it was dark outside. We then found the old door in the basement and carried it upstairs when no one was around to see.

Now I stood there, shifting from one foot to the other, and I asked what he was planning to do that day, trying to pose the question casually, as if it were no big deal, and he responded that he planned to spend the day at Santa Marinella. That information stung me because we had never returned there since our first date, though we often talked about it. I hesitated a moment, not knowing what to say. I didn't want him to see that it bothered me he was going there, but thinking he might ask me to come along, I stood there with a smile on my face. He just cocked his head so I shrugged my shoulders and told him I needed to get back home.

Instead of offering to accompany me to the bus stop, which he had always done before, he gave me another hug, turned around and walked across the room, then he lay down on his futon and shut his eyes as I turned to walk out the door. I glanced back one more time before closing the door behind me to see him staring up at the ceiling with a strange smile on his face. I never did ask him about the building in Trastevere from last night. A sense of unease tingled inside of me and I didn't want to know. I took the bus back to my apartment, and feeling completely drained, I spent the rest of the day in bed reading books until it was time to sleep.

My phone rang early the next morning, and it was his voice on the other end asking if I would come over, so I convinced myself that my fears of yesterday had been unfounded and things between us were fine. I got dressed and took the bus over to his apartment, and from there we walked around town a bit before stopping for coffee at our favorite place. My hope that his jovial mood would return was not realized, however, but instead he sat there quietly, as if he was in another world.

This day was a particularly beautiful late summer day, and the city was more empty than usual due to ferragosto, the summer vacation. Although it was hot, I could feel a slight breeze blow across the chairs that were stacked up in front of the empty restaurants, and I could smell some of the fresh air that is normally tamped down by heavy traffic. Few coffee shops were open during the holiday, but this one, located near the coliseum, remained open for tourists.

I ordered an espresso, and the owner gave me a generous smile reserved for repeat customers. The tables were all vacant, so I selected a location beneath the overhang right next to the window to better shield us from the sun. In this way we sat there and watched the tourists begin to line up against the forum entrance waiting for the ticket booth to open, and I couldn't help but notice that the entire time we sat there, my boyfriend seemed to freeze up every few seconds, put his coffee cup down on the table, adjust his glasses, pick his cup up again and press it to his lips for a few seconds, and then repeat the process. Although his glasses were the same black frames he had worn since I met him, they suddenly seemed large and heavy, and they must have been very uncomfortable since they kept sliding off his face and making him squint as if his prescription were suddenly wrong. I noticed that the glasses were also broken and one side had black tape winding around the hinges to keep the parts together.

I looked more closely at him from across the table, and it was then I realized that despite the fact we had spent a lot of time together over the summer, I still knew so little about him. He never spoke about his family and he never fully explained why he was going to school in Rome instead of Athens. He lived in a modest apartment and had enough money for food, but he had very few possessions.

I knew one thing about him, however, and that was he owned several very expensive cameras that he took everywhere he went, and he made some money shooting portraits in the Piazza di Spagna. He developed his own film in the back of a friend's photography shop, and his pictures were achingly beautiful in the way he could shape the core essence of a person's being by highlighting a tilt of the head, a crooked brow, a pouting lip.

One day he made a series of photographs of young boys who posed for their portraits with a cocky, don't mess-with-me attitude directed at the camera lens, then he took a series of images of a group of young girls, who posed carefully and rigidly for the camera. Although he never seemed to pay much attention to people with whom he was talking face-to-face, from behind the camera lens he could see deep inside a person's soul.

He was meticulous in the shooting and development of his photographs, but then he would leave them strewn carelessly across his apartment and he never minded if they were stepped on or had coffee spills across them. I encouraged him to look for a gallery or a restaurant that would agree to display them in a small exhibition, but he would just shrug his shoulders and laugh. I loved that about him but I also knew we had no future together.

The end of summer was about to arrive, and it would soon be time to leave Rome. I needed to return to Boston to finish college, and my boyfriend would eventually go back to Athens, and I would never see him again. He claimed he wanted to stay in Rome to work in the film industry, despite the fact that he had made no contacts, had not worked as an intern, and he did nothing to promote his photography—beautiful as it was, it was never displayed outside his apartment.

I therefore began to find myself avoiding his phone calls and cutting our time together shorter and shorter. I had lost all my friends by now, and felt very much alone. I longed for the carefree, happy friendships I saw all around me, the laughing couples, the families dining together, the happy, chatting, easy joy. How did I miss all of that? I was definitely ready to go home.

A few days before my flight, I took the bus over to my boyfriend's apartment one last time, without calling him first. By now he almost never went out anyway, despite his discomfort about the bedbugs in his apartment, so I knew he would be home. Once I entered the foyer of his apartment building, though, things seemed different, so I ran up the stairway suddenly nervous, wondering what I would say to him. My happiness at my impending return home began to twist into sadness as I thought about how we had met that cold day in Piazza Navona, and now it was the end of the summer, and I was leaving.

I ran down the hall and saw his door ajar, so I pushed it open to find a completely empty room. At first I thought I had entered the wrong apartment so I turned around to quickly leave, but I looked back again because I knew it was the correct door, it was the right place. I leaned up against the door and refocused my eyes on the emptiness in front of me. I walked into the kitchen, then into the bathroom, seeing that everything was gone. The floor was dirty, with some pieces of trash left behind, scattered around. I returned to the living area, where I noticed five empty San Pellegrino bottles lined up beneath the window next to where the futon was.

My boyfriend had clearly made a hasty departure. I felt dizzy and didn't know what to do. Since he didn't ever talk to any of his neighbors, there was no one I could ask about him, so I headed down to the superintendent's apartment and knocked on the door, but nobody answered. The emptiness of the apartment seemed to spill into a larger emptiness that covered the entire apartment building, as I stood there, completely still; it was so quiet.

After a few more minutes of waiting around in the foyer, I turned and walked out the front door. I spent some time walking up and down the street, as if I might see him returning, realizing he had made a mistake, bringing his things back. It was all a mistake! We would laugh. I considered walking to the train station, but what did I expect to find? I circled around and around the neighborhood until I became increasingly more comfortable with the idea that he would not reappear. I was, after all, leaving too, so what did I expect? With that thought, I caught the bus back to my apartment.

———

Two days later, in the very early morning, I took the shuttle to the Rome airport. I walked across the street one last time while my mind buzzed with the sights and sounds of the now retreating city, the beautiful buildings rising up from ancient foundations and the staccato bites of Italian words punctuated by the sounds of the streets. The shuttle transfer to the terminal was packed with people but I managed to wedge myself in a corner seat and lean my face out the open window. It was 6 a.m. and a light rain just finished, so I breathed in the smell of dampness that rose up off the street and mingled with the exhaust fumes to create a pungent odor not found anywhere else in the world.

The bus squealed to a halt in front of Terminal Five and disgorged its passengers into a long line that formed outside the building and snaked inside to the ticket counter. Three hours later, I was settled on the plane and the jagged edges of my sadness smoothed out into a sense of calm. I was finally going home.

I had arranged to stay with my sister in Boston for a few days until school started, and then I planned to move back into the dorms for one final year of college. It was early morning when I left Rome, and it was early morning when my plane arrived in Boston with just enough light in the sky to watch the plane descend outside the city. The Boston airport is such that right when you think you are too close to the water, a runway appears out of nowhere and the wheels touch the pavement. You can't see the wheels, but you can hear them squeaking and feel the plane moving forward on terra firma. I love seeing the water come so close to the plane and then slip away behind it. The water is always choppy in Boston with waves swirling around bringing up white foam into the mist, but as we approached the runway, the water flattened out and I saw trees, then buildings in the distance.

Finally, I could hear the breaks squeal and I lurched forward just a bit in my seat as the plane strained to slow down. We were traveling on the runway at the velocity of a slow automobile, and then the plane finally stopped just short of the side of the airport terminal. The door of the hangar was wrenched open and the moveable walkway attached to the side of the plane.

I stretched my legs and began to think about gathering together all my belongings. I was too tired to jockey for position in the narrow aisle and press against all the people standing and waiting for the airplane doors to be opened so we could exit the plane in one big group. Instead, I sat there checking the front seat pockets and looking through my purse one last time to make sure I had my passport, wallet and phone as people started slowly filing out.

Once the plane was almost empty, I pulled my yellow sweatshirt on and put my hood up over my head just as a burst of cold air came down on me from the overhead knobs. I tried to stand up but I was hunched beneath the overhead storage, so I crawled across the seats until I was in the aisle and could reach my bag, which I slung over my shoulder and walked forward toward the front of the plane. I knew my sister would be standing outside the gate waiting for me, but I didn't hurry.

"Thank you, thank you," I said to the flight attendants as I stepped into the walkway. The pilot was still in his seat, marking things off on a spreadsheet. A huge line had formed at customs, so I joined the back of the line and slowly crept forward until I was able to hand my passport to the agent, who looked at me smiling and said in a soft southern accent "Welcome home." So it was a southern accent in Boston that I first heard back in the United States.

Next, I worked my way to the baggage claim area where I saw my sister smiling and waving.

I suddenly realized how tired I was, but I knew that we still had to take the T to Back Bay before I could rest in a real bed. I was so tired I envisioned myself lying down on the floor of the airport curled up in the corner for a few hours where I wouldn't be in the way, and then I could have someone carry me home. Instead, I gave my sister a big hug and we waited for my luggage on the conveyor belt. Then we dragged both suitcases toward the public transportation signs until we arrived at the T stop. It wasn't too far to my sister's apartment, where I finally collapsed in bed.

———

"Look at what I found," my sister said, pointing toward the table. I had just walked into the kitchen later that evening after having slept all afternoon. I had fallen asleep in the daylight and woke up in dusk, which was discombobulating. I looked over to where my sister was pointing, and saw my violin case.

"Why do you have that?" I asked as I clicked open the latch to find my violin beneath the cloth.

"Mom asked me to keep it, she was cleaning out the attic and thought you'd want it back."

"Tomorrow I'll buy some music," I responded happily. I hadn't played my violin in two years.

"How are Mom and Dad doing, anyway?" I

asked, after popping a cracker in my mouth. I didn't realize how hungry I was.

"I guess they're OK," she said, shrugging her shoulders. "I don't see them that often since I have so much work to do."

My sister turned to ask me a question, "So what happened to this boyfriend you told me about a few months ago? How come you never said anything else about him?"

Suddenly I became embarrassed and shrugged my shoulders. I didn't know where to begin. Our relationship had ended so abruptly that I wondered if it had even happened in the first place, or did I just dream the whole thing? He and I had never really talked about any of this, about us.

"Is something wrong?" my sister asked.

"No, nothing," I said evasively. My stomach suddenly churned with nausea.

"Actually, I don't really feel well," I responded and pushed away the plate of food my sister had just set on the table in front of me. "I think I'll just lie back down a bit, it must be the jet lag."

I got up from the table and tried not to look at the slight frown on my sister's face.

The next morning I was feeling better so I decided to walk down to the music shop on Beacon Street. Although I hadn't been there in a long time, I remembered its general location and I thought the long walk would help me get reacquainted with the city. I found the store in the lower level of one of the brownstone buildings, next to Steve's Ice Cream. I entered the building, turned left, and went down the steep flight of stairs that led to the basement shop, where the narrow interior was filled with rows of shelves that held music for all different instruments. Further back in the shop the interior opened up into a larger space where one entire wall was hung with violins, violas and cellos while a series of tall armoires lined another wall with velvet-lined drawers that held bows for all the stringed instruments. Back in the front of the store, I decided to buy the sheet music for Faurè's *Berceuse*, which I had never played before.

By the time I returned to my sister's apartment, I felt sick again and was shaky and weak, so I decided to go back to bed.

"What is wrong?" my sister asked, peeking her head into my room later that evening when she returned from the grocery store.

"I don't know, but I'm so tired, I get so tired, maybe it is just all the changes from coming back home," I responded. My sister didn't look convinced, but wished me good night and turned out the light. I wasn't convinced either, but I didn't know what else to think.

The next day I enrolled in my classes and moved

into my dorm room. I was relieved to find out that as a senior, I had a single room, which I quickly filled with cheap furniture and lots of books. The weeks moved into fall that settled into the city to create beautifully chilly mornings and warm afternoons. The nights were beginning to get colder and the darkness came sooner. It was so different from Rome, which is darker than Boston because all the stores are covered with metal gates pulled down over the windows that block out any residual light. In Rome, electricity is expensive, so lights are turned on and off every time you enter and exit a room, but in Boston, lights stay on and pour forth from windows, street lamps, signs and shop fronts.

"Can I live with you instead of in the dorm?" I asked my sister one evening. I turned to face her from her living room couch where I was ensconced in a blanket and leaning against two pillows studying for an exam. She looked at me closely, clearly puzzled.

"Don't you want to hang out with your friends?" she asked. "This is your senior year, and you haven't even gone out with any of them."

"I know, but right now I don't feel well," I responded, "and I just want more of a home." At that point I started to cry.

"Of course you can live with me," she responded, looking alarmed.

I had already thought about how this would

work out. My sister was spending long hours in the library finishing her research project, so I knew I would have the apartment to myself most of the day, and her living room was an ideal place to study with a desk next to the window that was covered with plants. I pointed across the room and said, "I could push your plants to one side and put my computer there."

"That should work," she responded.

After careful calculation, I had realized that I would actually finish all my required coursework in December, so I could graduate early and look for a job in the spring. That way I could get a refund on part of my housing fees. My decision to graduate in December turned out to be prescient. By early October I was still feeling tired and weak, so I went to see a doctor and found out that I was four months pregnant. I was floored by this news, which swept my memories back to the early summer days in Rome that seemed so long ago. My sister was less shocked than I was; perhaps she suspected this all along. So I spent the fall with my sister, doing all the things we never did together when we were young. We ate pizza and ice cream. We walked the length of the city from the North End all the way down Beacon Street to Fenway. We spent long hours at the Fine Arts Museum. Neither of us spoke about the baby, we just went along each day waiting and wondering.

CHAPTER EIGHTEEN

Folly x 2 and
the Carpenter's Square

The line of nature is curved, curled, spiraled, collapsed in upon itself and simultaneously expanded outward toward infinity, and it is therefore incalculable. The line of man is instead carefully measured against the terror of the incalculable, and in this way it becomes a line of the known world, a line from which human existence can be measured.

Thus, the architect of the human world is a God with a framing square, a ruler, and a compass. The compass charts the heavens, the ruler measures time and space that exist both in the heavens and on earth, while the carpenter's square frames the earthly realm. The existence of the cardinal points creates an axis along the ninety-degree angle of the square that confirms our reality to us, and so the fear of the unknown is abated through *normae* and *regulae*.

When I asked Jack, who is now one month shy of age nineteen, if he feels normal, he responded that he doesn't know what that means. The rules that govern our daily lives are inconsequential to him—why go to school, why sleep at night, why take medicine, why are such things even expected?

In fact, he was in a bad mood because I had just asked that question, and so he scowled at me and stomped out of the room. I heard him in the living room talking on the phone, arranging a night out with friends. A plan must have been agreed upon because he went to sit on the sofa and he stared at his phone until eventually I heard a car pull up in front of the house and Jack shuffled out the front door, slamming it behind him.

I wanted to trail behind him and remind him that he should be home by 10 p.m. But number 10 is always the rule he breaks. The rule of 10. Jack returned from Ohio several months ago and now that he has nothing to do all day, he doesn't find it necessary to stay awake during the day-time and sleep at night.

I went into the living room and peeked out the side window while standing slightly behind the curtains. I saw Jack walking purposefully away from the house toward the car, and when he opened his friend's car door, music poured out into the air and energized him and he began to shake his head to the beat while swinging his long body into the car, one leg and then the other leg, and finally the arm that closed the door behind him. The two of them drove off, laughing together. I didn't hear the laugh from behind the closed window, of course, but I could see it. A laughing face tilts slightly upward, with the mouth open into a big smile, and the chest heaves as air goes in and out of the mouth rapidly, and this allows the sound that originates in the voice box to rise up and issue forth. I noticed that Jack's friend drove down the street too fast, and then they were gone.

The evening turned to night and I left Jack's bedroom light on and went to bed. I woke up at 5:45 a.m. and crawled out of bed and stumbled into the foyer. The front door was still unlocked, his bedroom door was open, and his light was still on. The bed was empty. Off in the distance I heard an ambulance siren, so I went into the living room and stared out the large picture window. In the front yard were three baby skunks digging in the dirt, and I thought to myself that now solves the mystery of why my front yard always has small, shallow holes scattered around it at random intervals.

I continued to stare out the window for about forty minutes until the sun began to come up in the sky, and then I heard in the distance the soft sounds of lyre strings being plucked, and I squinted upward until I could almost see Apollo riding across the sky in his golden chariot, pulling the sun behind him. The sun must not have been very heavy because Apollo's golden horses galloped with ease while Apollo himself was standing in front of the seat holding the reigns in both of his hands. If I were closer, I might have been able to see him laughing as his white robes flapped in the wind made by his movement.

The sound of the lyre turned into a second ambulance siren, and I went back to bed and lay there until my alarm went off at 7:30 a.m. I sprung out of bed and lurched into the bathroom, clipping the doorframe with my shoulder. I fought the urge to check Jack's bedroom again... should I check his bedroom? I should check his bedroom first, and then take a shower, I decided. No, I should take a shower first because during my shower I would be able to consider the possibility that he is home rather than knowing definitively that he is not.

———————

Armed with a carpenter's square, we think we can know the unknowable. We want to learn the mysteries of the universe, yet our starting point for all this knowledge springs from the numbers that form the circle, square, and triangle, 1, 2, 3, 5, 8, 13. We have a long way to go.

———————————

I decided to take a shower first, so I turned on the water and waited until it heated up before stepping into the bathtub. "There will be three good things for today," I announced to myself out loud. Number one is hot water. With no poison, I laughed, as an afterthought. Once I was in the shower, I stood there and watched the water falling down on me like steamy rain, and I began to think about that September afternoon when I was in my living room playing the violin while Jack was being arrested. Not knowing what was happening allowed me to play my violin, just like not knowing where Jack is now has allowed me to linger in the hot shower.

Now my thoughts began to shift to an earlier moment on that day in September, that day over a year ago. I thought back to a few minutes before I started playing the violin, when I was standing in the living room with my violin case open and I was putting rosin on my bow. Jack had come into the living room at that moment, that moment being about forty minutes before he took the keys to the car and drove off—he came into the living room and he was crying and I could tell that he had been drinking and he asked me a question that I never answered. He walked up to me and I was angry because it was a Sunday afternoon and he was drunk, and then he asked me why I never told him who his father was. I should have been prepared for this question, but I wasn't. I should have figured out an answer before this, but I didn't. Instead, I turned to him and told him that I would tell him the next day because he wouldn't remember anything on that day anyway.

He walked out of the living room and into the kitchen, and I started playing the violin. After a while, I remembered that I heard the clinking of the car keys. These were the keys I had begun to hide from him when he started sneaking out at night, but since I left them on the counter that day, he picked them up, went out into the garage, and drove off in my car. I kept playing the violin a few more minutes so that I could finish the piece of music because I knew that when the day ended, I would never play the violin again, and at least I wanted to finish the Faurè.

I continued to stand in the shower, thinking about that September afternoon because it was on that day I realized I hadn't been able to escape my fate. When I'd left Rome those many years ago, I thought I could run away from it all. I could avoid its implications if I traveled back across the ocean to start a new life first in Boston and then in Oklahoma, where it wouldn't follow me. But that simply wasn't true.

———————

The line of nature is a spiral, and it was an imperfect spiral of DNA lurking in Jack's body that followed him from Rome to Oklahoma via Boston. What I hoped would be a straight line, a long line measured across the horizon from point A—Rome—to point B—Oklahoma—going only in one direction, was instead a circle where the point at which you begin to draw is an arbitrary point because the line will curve around and meet back again once the circle is completed, even if you never go back to Rome. That is when I knew what Jack would be burdened with from that day onward, and so I called and called and called his phone until I reached the police officer, relieved to hear his voice, and on that Sunday afternoon I lay down in the middle of my living room floor and buried my tears in the carpet.

———————

I finished my shower and got dressed quickly as the panic of not knowing where Jack was began to set in again, and I walked quickly down the hall and turned the corner to Jack's bedroom, where I saw the door still ajar and the light on. I peered around the doorframe to see the bed still empty. The remnants of moist shower heat turned cold on my skin and goose bumps suddenly erupted up and down my arms as my stomach churned. Just then, I heard the front door open and the dog started barking furiously but he calmed to a growl when he saw Jack. I heard Jack's footsteps as he walked through the living room and then he sauntered into his bedroom, not surprised to see me standing there.

"Can you make me breakfast?" he asked. I looked at his rumpled clothing and heard a car drive away from our house.

"Sure, but I have to leave in ten minutes, so go ahead into the kitchen and get the eggs out while I brush my hair," I responded, walking out of his room and back toward the bathroom.

A few minutes later, I came into the kitchen and put Jack's medicine out on the counter, trying not to look at him as he swallowed his pills. I turned toward the stove and cracked two eggs into the frying pan while thinking to myself that today he has taken his lithium. At this very moment, I imagined, the capsule was traveling down his esophagus like a steep slide at the water park, and splashing into his stomach. As I flipped the eggs over, I thought of the capsule first loosening and then breaking open so the lithium powder could slowly float out into his stomach and disperse, soaking into his gut before traveling upward through his blood stream to cross the blood-brain barrier and begin its task of plumping up Jack's gray matter like the rehydration of a giant piece of dried fruit. I carried the frying pan over to the counter and dumped the cooked eggs onto a plate next to the toast Jack had just finished buttering.

Then I grabbed my tote bag and walked out the garage door to my car. "I'll see you after work," I yelled on the way out. Maybe Jack will go to bed now and sleep soundly, I hoped. Maybe today his brain will get the rest it needs and his mind will rinse away all the dirty water, the neurotoxins, and allow the clean water to settle into his brain with sparkling clarity. As for me, I thought that if only I can count out numbers, count out the days like 1, 2, 3, 4, 5 and keep things nice and orderly while the medicine starts to work, Jack and I will be able to figure this shit out.

When I got home from work that evening, I walked around the house in a circle looking for Jack in all the rooms but leaving his bedroom last since I expected to find him there asleep. But his bed was empty. The house was completely quiet except for the soft padding of animal feet as my dog followed me around the house hoping for a walk. I went into the kitchen and walked straight over to the trash can. I flipped open the lid and dug deep into the trash with my fingers, rooting around the banana peels and coffee grounds until I found Jack's medicine folded into a napkin crumpled up and pushed halfway down the depth of the can. My heart sank into my stomach—why do I look for what I don't want to find?

I carefully studied the off-white oval-shaped pill that had two letters and an insignia stamped on it that looked like a backwards letter "a." The pill was still dry, with no debris stuck to it, so I put it in my mouth and swallowed it. I drank an entire glass of water and went over to my desk, pulled open a drawer, and found the black spiral notebook that I had been using for a year now to record Jack's medications and various treatment plans.

I turned to the first blank page located somewhere in the middle of the book and carefully wrote the date at the top of the page, then in the middle of the page I wrote the time and the name of the medicine and the dosage that I just took. I closed the notebook with a pen tucked inside of it, ready to write down more information when the time was right. Then I went into the living room and lay down on the sofa for a nap, thinking I would rest until Jack came home and then we would eat dinner together. The nap turned into a full night of heavy sleep, however, where

I tossed and turned all night long wrestling with a set of odd dreams.

The next morning I awoke with a start, feeling cold sweat across my forehead. I never heard Jack come home, nor did I hear my alarm go off. My phone was on the floor next to the sofa, facing upward where I could see the time was 8:40 a.m. and I had to be at work at 9 a.m., so I staggered up off the sofa, down to my bedroom, and rooted around in my closet to find an outfit to wear to work, settling on black pants and a black shirt.

I peered into his bedroom through the open door, but no Jack. Before I left the house, however, I went into the pantry and grabbed the bottle of pills that he was supposed to be taking, popped one in my mouth, and left the bottle on the counter so he wouldn't forget to take it when he returned home. Then I clicked on my computer and looked at my phone account to see when Jack's phone was last used, which was four hours ago. So, I knew definitively that at 4:50 a.m. Jack was still vertical to the earth, even though I didn't know where he was. I left the front door unlocked and closed the garage door behind me.

I returned home from work that evening to find Jack's medicine still sitting on the counter where I left it for him. The toaster was pushed to the edge of the counter and the bread bag was left open, so I knew he had been home. On the way to his bedroom, I looked out the sliding glass door to see his bicycle lying in the middle of the backyard. His bedroom door was now closed, so I slowly eased it open without knocking and tiptoed into the room, where I saw him lying sprawled across his bed, face down, clutching his phone in one hand while his other arm was wrapped around a pillow. I stared at his back long enough to see the rise of his ribs up and down, barely perceptible, but enough to know that he was breathing.

When he was a baby I would gently lay my hand on his back to make sure he was breathing, but now that he is older, I didn't want to risk waking him up. Since he seemed to be sleeping soundly, I decided to linger in his bedroom and look around a bit. Jack's bed was a futon that rested on a low wooden platform stained a dark brown color. The bed was positioned against one wall, and from there it stretched out into the middle of the room. On the far wall was a coat rack with a jumble of jackets, coats, and a bathrobe hanging from the hooks. I recognized only half the clothing.

On the opposite wall next to the window stood the large remnants of the spaceship cardboard taped together to form a large rectangular box secured with more tape to the wall. This was the sensory deprivation chamber. On a low table next to the cardboard rested a jumble of cameras, lenses, cords, chargers, batteries, cases, covers, and his computer with a cracked screen. The exterior of the computer was covered with black marker drawings.

Against the final wall, the wall that had the door where I just now entered his room, was another low table covered with a stack of books, crumpled pieces of paper, and a bookshelf that had been cleared away of all its books and filled with his shoes. The rest of his books lined the shelves in his bathroom closet, where all of his clothing lay in a large pile on the floor. On the bathroom counter was a container of lighter fluid and a pair of scissors.

I instinctively opened the window a crack to see if the screen was still there, and then I slid open the counter drawers and felt along the backside, checking for bottles. In the closet, I quickly ran my hands along the jackets to see if any bottles were tucked into the pockets, any money rolled up, small plastic bags, plastic pens taken apart, strange smells, film containers with tissues tucked in them, or tissues in the trash can with blood on them. I then came back out of the bathroom and looked around the bedroom one last time before leaving.

A notebook then caught my eye because of its placement right next to Jack's bed. It was covered in multicolored duct tape and had a pen tucked between the pages. I crept over to his bed while staring at his sleeping form, afraid of wakening him. Quietly I reached down and picked up the notebook, which I could see was half-filled with handwritten pages done in all different colors of pen and marker. Some pages were covered with drawings of stick figures, some of whom were laughing while others frowning, some were staring out of the book while others were running around the pages like book gremlins. I turned to the page with a date written at the top that corresponded with when Jack started college, and on that page I saw Jack had written this list:

1. Make sure to go to class.
2. Try to look interested even if I am not.
3. Make sure to smile at the teacher.
4. Sit next to one different student each day.
5. Show people that I care.

Jack stirred in his sleep, and I looked over at him and caught my breath in fear, but he didn't wake. I slowly bent down and placed his notebook at the exact spot where I found it, upside down and facing away from his bed.

I returned to the kitchen and went back into the pantry and starting sorting through the bottles on the shelf where I kept all of Jack's medicine, which included all the prescriptions he didn't take anymore. Because he never took anything regularly, yet I always refilled his prescriptions, we had an impressive stock of anti-depressants, mood stabilizers, anxiety medications and anti-psychotic pills, all different brands and strengths, all collected on the way to finding the perfect medicine cocktail, a goal that continued to elude Jack.

I remembered that I had taken one of Jack's pills yesterday and another one this morning before I went to work and I hadn't noticed anything different except for the weird dreams last night, but I did start with a low dose, I reasoned, so I now decided to double the dose and add a second medication. This way I could see if they kept me awake or allowed me to sleep with fewer vivid dreams, which I had found disturbing.

I got out the black spiral notebook that I had hidden beneath a pile of papers, skipped past the first half of the book where I had been recording Jack's symptoms, doctor's appointments, medications and supplements together with all the information I had gathered from the internet about the brain, and I found the same page I had written on yesterday. There I recorded today's date and time, together with a notation about my increase in medication and dosage, and I left a blank space so I could describe my impressions later on.

CHAPTER NINETEEN

Aristotle and the Queen of Cups

*"...the faculty by which, in waking hours, we
are subject to illusion when affected by disease, is
identical with that which produces illusory effects
in sleep."*

On Dreams, by Aristotle, c. 350 B.C.

When Jack wasn't building a spaceship or wandering through town in the middle of the night, he was perfecting his ability to lucid dream. Because many things fall out of the range of human expression in the waking world, he wanted to cultivate his life experiences in the dream world since he decided the waking world was too constrained by the categorization of facts, judgments and assessments that hampered his imagination. By lucid dreaming, he told me, he could control his thoughts and actions through orchestrating their location and narrative, and he could remember his dreams with great clarity once he woke up so they were no different from "reality."

The waking world is also constrained by a fixed expression of time, place, and motion. Aristotle said that time only exists if it can be measured as a rate of change or motion, and time can only be measured by a mind, which is needed to count it. By counting, one expresses an *arithmos kineseos* such that one two three four five six seven eight nine ten becomes a standard of measurement of movement with respect to calculating the "before" and the "after." Motion, then, is made visible by the movement of an object, so one can say that time is an ordering system that requires numerical calculation of the movement of some object in space.

In the dreaming world, however, time can stand still or move forward or backward, and because it is not measured in consistent intervals, it can also compress or expand. Therefore, the expression of time passing in a consistent way is "reality," so in the waking world, Jack can check his watch, wait, and check it again to see the minute hand adjust slightly to account for the passing of time. In the dreaming world, time doesn't move in a consistent pattern, so Jack began to wear his watch to bed in order to tell the difference. This method worked for a while, until he began to experiment with the use of black ink designs drawn onto the back of his hand, which provided a focal point for the observation of consistent designs as a reality check.

Because there is no external time axis in our universe, time moves with respect to a time reference, which we base upon the "now." If we theorize that time flows continuously, we feel time moving on the time axis in such a way that allows us to only know the past and present but not the future, and so we must select a course of action from the infinite possibilities learned from our past, and then follow that path into the future.

Time in the past is "frozen," i.e. that which cannot be changed, but can time in the future change? Or, are events already determined, fixed, but just not knowable to us until we experience them? I'm not certain what is true, but I just want everyone to know that in a tarot card reading I had many years ago, I was told that I was going to be involved in a very serious car accident while driving a blue car. Since I moved to Oklahoma, which I dreamed about during my childhood, I have been doing my very best to avoid driving blue cars, but you are all my witnesses here—so if I forget about this tarot reading and slip behind the steering wheel of a blue car and this prognostication comes to pass, I am telling you right here and now that it isn't a mere coincidence.

Anyway, we use this distortion on the time axis to our advantage by expressing our ability to make decisions that will shape our future. In the dream world, however, time is not revealed on the time axis, and the past and present are just as mutable as the future, so one can live with no future fears and past regrets, the ultimate freedom.

In the dream world, Jack can fly through space. Since there is no definition of space outside of our universe, space must be measured relative to objects, and here we can say the universe is made of space-time, which is defined as the laws that relate momentum and matter. Through time, humans have yearned to fly, to escape, like Daedalus, or to theorize a new way of looking at the world, like Leonardo da Vinci.

In 1502, when Leonardo was fifty years old, he drew an aerial view map of the Chiana Valley of central Italy. Leonardo da Vinci saw the valley as if he were a bird flying over it, but how? Did he dream it? Surely he would have climbed one of the many surrounding mountains, and while standing at the precipice of one of nature's cliffs, he would have made sketches of the valley drawn at a raking angle of around 45%, which he could have recalculated to 90% and adjusted the perspective points of his drawing to achieve the appearance of looking straight down upon the valley.

In this way, Leonardo da Vinci created a mathematical study with profound philosophical implications because he could replicate a view of nature that a human standing on earth could never have seen at that time-space juncture of 1502. It was an image of the earth that at that time was within the purview of God alone.

It is because of these sorts of things that Jack included the dreaming into his life experiences and did not privilege the waking world in his version of reality. Therefore, his mutable vantage point for observable reality is substantially different from the reality of most people.

———————

One night that December I dreamed I went to an amusement park to visit a fantasy-themed house that I had wanted to see for a long time. The theme park was located across a large lake, and to get there I had to walk along the water's edge and curve around the lake since it was too cold and deep to swim across. The shoreline was covered with beautiful, round, mossy pebbles, and the water was so clear I decided to wade into it. I walked through the shallow part of the water, holding up my blue dress to keep it dry, and there I spotted a large Styrofoam cup floating further out in the lake; it was a 32-ounce Big Gulp. So I waded into a deeper area where I could reach it, and I brought it back to shore. I looked around for a trash can but none was nearby, so

I regrettably realized that I had to carry the cup with me, since I didn't want to litter.

It was late afternoon and the theme park was about to close, so it was emptying out of visitors as I entered, and while I walked away from everyone else, the park grew quieter with each moment. The streets were bathed in a beautiful golden sunlight and caused me to linger down the walkway that led to the fantasy house. And so I walked through the amusement park and enjoyed its exquisite beauty, its fictive decrepit agedness, its fabricated reality, with its picturesque streets and no traffic.

Along the way I passed the remaining visitors going in the opposite direction from me, all heading toward the exit. All together they looked like one giant allegory of tired joy, with their faces revealing a unified sense of accomplishment and spent satisfaction. They were young, old, rich and poor, fat and thin. They had come from near and far and were strangers to each other but were bound together forever in this shared venture on this same day of their diverse lives. Their memories, if merged together, would form one complete, universal park experience.

As I walked further into the park, the remaining people I passed were the park employees emptying the trash cans and sweeping the streets of the sticky candy wrappers, cans, plastic cups and napkins. Finally I was able to throw away the

Styrofoam cup I had been carrying along with me! The trash can featured the results of an orgy of junk food, a no-holds-barred consumption of all the most unhealthy things that call to us like a sweet song; a song we resist outside the walls of the amusement park, but we allow to take over on this one special day, or on many days, for those people who bought a season pass.

Two of the employees were tying a trash bag together, two hands on one side of the bag and two hands on the other side, each holding a plastic flap and twining it in through the other flaps to create a knot. The couple laughed together as their hands brushed against each other, and when the bag was tied, the man hoisted it up over his shoulder and together they walked toward the maintenance building barely visible behind the candy shop.

I consulted the ornate street sign and made one more left turn, where I saw, at the edge of the amusement park, a large, rambling, multi-level tree house built in the Victorian style with a topsy-turvy arrangement of walkways, porches, and rooms all cascading downward from the very top of the tree to the ground. Behind the tree I saw a meadow, where a gentle breeze was kicking up that created a waving movement across the tall grass and flowers. The sun was now resting on the horizon and it blinded my distant view so I couldn't see the edge of the amusement park, just golden light reflected back at me.

In order to explore this tree house, I had to climb a series of ladders to the top floor, crawl through a low door, and work my way down what seemed to be six interior floors. Once I got to the top and walked inside the house, I saw rows of rooms down a broad, long hallway with at least six rooms on either side, which was puzzling to me because the house didn't look that big from the exterior. I peeked into a few of the rooms and found that each room followed a different theme, with crooked walls and cozy furniture, which was oddly familiar and reassuring to me, probably because I had read all the Winnie the Pooh books when I was young.

Only after I looked into the third room did I notice a man sitting at a table, wearing a costume and powdered wig from the eighteenth century. He was waiting, I assumed, for visitors to arrive even though the amusement park was now closed. I surmised that each room featured a different historical character, and so I walked into the next room and there I saw a man dressed like Aristotle. He was seated at a wooden table drinking coffee from a chunky white diner mug and chatting with three other men who were also wearing long robes similar to his. As I looked at all four men, in one instant I realized, I don't know how, but I realized that it actually was Aristotle, and I felt that truth wash over me and settle deeply into my heart.

Suddenly, I was struck with the thought that this chance encounter offered me a wonderful opportunity; I now had the possibility of unlocking history once and for all because I could ask Aristotle all the questions I had always wondered about, all the things I tried to understand while spending my life pouring through books and research materials and archival documents. So now I needed only to ask, and to receive the answers to life's questions. Where should I begin?

I started my conversation with the statement: "You know, I am very interested in this architecture."

He looked up and responded: "I know," while nodding kindly in the affirmative.

I wasn't sure what to say next, so I looked out the window and noticed, much to my surprise, that despite all the steps I had just climbed, we were at ground level looking out at the meadow.

Amazed, I pointed this out to Aristotle, and he looked up again and responded with a slow smile, "I know."

And this is when I woke up, before I could ask my third question! The third question was going to be the real deal, the question that was going to provide the answer that would unlock the foundation principles of human knowledge from which I could extrapolate an infinite understanding of the entire universe. But I had missed my chance! Now I will never understand.

———————

But Jack is different. Because Jack is a lucid dreamer, he has traveled widely and spoken with a great number of enlightened beings, both living and dead. Needless to say, he has already met Aristotle and heard the answer to the third question, but he cannot explain the answer to me because no words exist that can express such ideas that lie outside the capacity of the human mind to think them—these ideas are not only too vast and too complex, but they are also constantly mutable, so once you think you understand something, then you don't!

Given how grand all this knowledge is—why, then, does it make me so sad to see Jack slip away from the carnal world, when in fact he is still alive?

CHAPTER TWENTY

The Wheel of Fortune

"Sēp ognora mimovo, loco stabili n trovo"

-Lorenzo "Spirito"
Gualtieri, *Libro delle Sorti*, 1482

The weight of what was happening to Jack loomed across the winter. Many evenings I sat alone in my living room next to the fireplace, piling in more firewood and opening more beer or wine while ignoring holiday invitations and Christmas cards. On one particular evening, after I had finished one bottle of wine and uncorked a second bottle, I suddenly got the idea that, instead of sitting around pondering so many questions of what to do, I thought I would try to divine some answers by consulting my sorting book.

I had bought this sorting book when I lived in Rome as a college student, at the old book dealer's stall at the Porta Portese antique market that I visited every Sunday morning, only I didn't really buy it, but the book dealer gave it to me. It was a Sunday during the springtime when I was in Italy, and since it wasn't cold anymore I decided to walk to the market instead of taking the bus there.

The walk took me longer than I thought, so it was late morning by the time I arrived. When I got there I headed straight to the area where the book dealers had lined up their stalls in three crooked rows, just like every Sunday, and I rounded the corner to see my friend stationed at his bookstall, just like every Sunday. When he saw me he smiled and waved me over with his left hand, waving his hand with his fingers pointing downwards like Italians do, and in his right hand he held up an old book bound together with thick leather that was stitched up along the sides.

He knew that I was in Italy to study art history, so he often set aside art books for me to look at. Sometimes I would buy them, when I had money. On this particular day he had a big grin on his face, and he handed me this book with a flourish, knowing that it would make me happy because it was extra special. I looked at the book and saw that the leather was old and stiff and bumpy in parts, with the top corner stained and curled up slightly. I opened the book and found some beautiful illustrations done in tempera paint next to some old script that appeared to give a list of questions, then some names of kings, and then some dice charts with animal pictures in boxes, and then several pages of little sonnets written at the end. Some pages had round charts, like zodiac signs, but without the star patterns.

I didn't know what to do with the book since I didn't have any money to buy it, so I held it out awkwardly toward my friend waiting for a cue from him, and he just laughed with his toothless mouth open and shooed me away with the book still in my hand. I started to speak but he was already distracted, engrossed in conversation with an older woman. That was how he always acted, laughing and talking with me while his eyes constantly darted across the crowd looking for other people he knew, friends of his from long ago who had a stronger pull on him than I did. Yet, even though it didn't seem like he was ever really paying attention to me, when I came to see him every Sunday he always knew exactly what type of book I was looking for and had it ready for me.

This book was different, though, so when I got back to my apartment I began to leaf through the pages, and on the first page I read that the book was written in 1482 by a man named Lorenzo Gualtieri who lived in the hill town of Perugia and was paid to copy and recopy books all by hand, and he seemed to be particularly proud of this book, which he called a *sortilegium*.

From what I could tell, Lorenzo wrote the book as a gift for the mercenary soldier Braccio Baglione, who wanted to be seen as a *gentiluomo,* and so Braccio used this book to help him make decisions about his family and his business. The book must have told a story, I thought, but I wasn't sure what to do with it.

So the following Sunday I returned to Porta Portese because I wanted to ask my friend more about the book, but on that day his book stall was still shuttered even though the market was open and crowded with people. I asked the vendor next to him if he had seen my friend, but he just shrugged his shoulders and turned his lips downward. I returned a few more Sundays, but by then school was over and I had made plans to return home. I packed the book in my luggage, but once I got back to the United States, I forgot about it.

And so here I was, twenty years later, pulling the dusty old book off my living room bookshelf and propping it up on a sofa cushion so I could turn the brittle pages. I now recognized that the pages were made of vellum and painted with fine temperas in the style of Raphael. The sheets of paper were thick and appeared to be folded in half and stitched together with thick cotton thread to form the binding of the book, which was then covered with the leather that I remembered, curved and stained. I carefully opened the book to the first page and saw a beautiful hand-painted image of the Wheel of Fortune with the inscription: "Sēp ognora mimovo, loco stabili n trovo," which loosely translates as: "with every movement I make, I cannot find a stable place." I knew it was the Wheel of Fortune because the image had four figures clinging to different parts of a large wooden wheel that was placed in the center of the page. The figure perched on the top of the wheel appeared to be seated and was dressed in imperial clothing, but instead of a crown he had the ears of a donkey. Above his head was the inscription "I rule."

As the wheel began to turn clock-wise, an unfortunate soul could be seen falling head first toward the ground, where a third figure was being crushed beneath the moving wheel while proclaiming: "I ruled!"—the words of which I heard out loud in my living room. I tried to dart out of the way of the moving wheel, and that was when I saw the tall, handsome, blond-haired youth, who looked just like Jack, clinging to the rim on the opposite side, where the wheel was turning upward, and then I heard him loudly declare: "I will rule!" He looked at me and laughed mockingly, and when I saw his face completely I knew without a doubt that it was Jack.

I looked above the wheel, and there I saw a cluster of questions, so I read through them until I found the one I wanted answered: "Will my son's health improve?" From my question sprang a response: "Se volete sapere se la salute di tuo figlio migliorerà, và al Re Artù." To find out, then, I had to go see King Arthur, so I flipped through the book to the page where I saw King Arthur dressed as a brave warrior; he was a king who battled both man on earth and beasts from the Otherworld. I introduced myself and told him a bit about Jack, but he abruptly interrupted me and pointed to his right and directed me to "va al segno del alicorno."

I didn't know why he wouldn't answer my question, so I continued through the book until I saw a page with an image of a unicorn, or *alicorno*, painted in the middle, surrounded by a dice chart. I reached into my pocket and felt three dice, so I pulled them out of my pocket and I knelt down to roll all three of them across the ground. I rolled 5–3–1. I looked up at the unicorn now standing above me, and the unicorn looked first at the dice and then at me, and I sensed that he was directing me to find the *montone*, but what was a montone? I skipped through the book to the next section and looked at each page until I saw the name written above an image of a ram, and I looked back at the unicorn for confirmation that I had the correct page, and he nodded up and down and said to me without speaking: "Va a la spera del Montone, dentro al fiume Frigio."

To find the ram, then, I had to go to a river

called the Frigio River, but I didn't know where that was although it sounded really cold, so I started walking north and I walked and walked, and I gradually started to feel more and more tired and could not keep my eyes open. I stumbled along until finally, after walking a very long time, I looked up and saw a beautiful ram standing at the edge of a river, and he was shining like he was in a dream. I suddenly knew this river was the Phrygian River, although I didn't know how I knew that, and I began to climb down the embankment toward the ram, and the water that splashed up from the river lingered ice cold from the winter and I watched the clear liquid pour over rocks and hurtle downstream.

I looked up and across the river to see a vast flat plain with a few scruffy plants growing against the wind. I seemed to be on a plateau somewhere in Anatolia, but it was completely devoid of any sign of human intervention, which meant we were in ancient times before the region was inhabited and before it was described in the *Iliad*. Right then the ram slowly turned to look at me, and since he could not speak I looked into his eyes and I knew what I needed to do—I had to cross the river and walk down some distance where I would find the Prophet David, the King.

So I began to look for a way to cross the river, but as I wandered along trying to find a spot where the water was more still or where the river was narrower, I grew more and more tired with each step I took. I saw a part of the river that appeared shallower, so I plunged into the frigid water right there hoping I wouldn't sink to the bottom, all the while trying desperately to remind myself that I had to ask King David for his 20th triplet verse—it had to be that one in particular because that was the one that would provide me the answer to my question. How I knew to ask for that verse, I did not know.

The cold water revived me, but only briefly because once I set foot on the opposite shore and started walking again, my aching feet immediately reminded me of how tired I was, how I had walked such a long way, but I knew I couldn't turn back. My mind began to lose its focus so I tried really hard to think straight not only so that I could follow through with the directions and ask for the correct triplet, but also so that once I heard it, I would remember it in order to know what to do once I got back at home.

I walked along the shore until King David finally appeared before me, old but still handsome, with traces of his regal bearing worn down by life's missteps. My visit with him was very short because he did not even introduce himself or ask me who I was; there was no small talk. Instead he abruptly turned to me and looked into both my eyes simultaneously in order to make me understand the gravity of his gentle but firm warning:

"Nō continuare su questa strada o troppo si ammalano anche tu." I translated his words as: "do not continue on this path, or you will get sick too." I had better get home quickly, I thought to myself, and so I turned back from the river and hurried home. I'll be safe at home, I thought to myself in my dream, but when I woke the next morning, I remembered none of this story.

CHAPTER TWENTY-ONE

The World

It is February, maybe March. Although I am not sure of what month it is exactly, I do know that the Christmas season has come and gone and it is somewhat past the beginning of the new year because spring is just starting to think about when to emerge. This year we did not drive up to Boston for the holidays. Instead, I planned to have a small Christmas celebration at home, but that never happened.

I walk into the kitchen and look at the wall calendar where all the days are listed in four rows of seven squares, but that number chart doesn't help me to know what today is. Furthermore, the calendar is from the wrong year anyway because it says "December" above a picture of a snow-covered golf course, so I take it off the hook and throw it into the trash.

I look around the kitchen, trying to find something to rest my eyes on that doesn't seem to move around so much and make me dizzy. I think that maybe I just need to sit down for a bit and keep my eyes closed, so I sit on the bar stool and rest my head on the counter, closing my eyes to test that theory out. Although the objects go away, the echoes of their shapes and colors are now swirling around inside my eyelids, still making me feel sick.

Furthermore, my right leg is shaking just a bit and it keeps bumping into the side of the counter, so I hold onto my thigh with my hand and squeeze it a bit, but that doesn't help much. I reach down to grab my foot and move it back from the counter so the rhythmic bumping sound goes away.

"I need to figure this out," I say to myself, and my voice startles me because I didn't realize I was talking out loud. My dog barks twice in the living room window; someone must be walking past the house. I don't remember the last time I took him out to pee, maybe that is what he is wanting.

It was last November when I knew I couldn't take much more stress so I took two weeks off work, which included the week of Thanksgiving, so part of that week didn't really count. I had about two months of unused vacation time, and since Christmas was coming soon, I wanted to be prepared. I was nervous about how Christmas would unfold given the events of last year, so I decided that this year I wanted the holiday season to come and go like it was no big deal, with just a small celebration.

I couldn't afford to buy plane tickets and I didn't like the idea of driving across the entire country and then possibly having to turn right back around to drive twenty-two hours straight through in order to check Jack into the hospital near our house. "That is ridiculous, this year is going to be different!" I had said to myself, but every time I tried to think about how it would be different, my head would start hurting. That's when I started taking an assortment of Jack's medicine, ratcheting up the dosages each week to see what would happen, doing my own medical experimentation.

I slowly lift my head up off the counter. Maybe if I just take a short nap, I think, I'll feel better and I'll be able to concentrate on some of the things I need to do for work. The office had called, I reminded myself, and Evelyn asked if I had any reports to submit before the end of the year, but I wasn't sure what that meant since the year already ended, so I didn't return her call.

I stand up from the bar stool and stagger out of the kitchen and into the dining room, where I see a stack of papers strewn across my desk, throbbing white sheets of bleached tree pulp. I was obviously looking for something last night and never cleaned up the mess. I look more closely at the papers to see that some are typed on letterhead while others have words jotted down by hand on lined paper, and some are in groups of printed papers stapled together. Since it is all a jumble, I decide that I should stack them into piles, making sure the sheets of paper are all lined up, which takes a bit of work because I have to tap them on the desk and then turn them sideways and tap them again, going round and round until they are all lined up, and then I set them in the corner of my desk.

The stack is now very neat and my desk looks good, I think, so I congratulate myself until I realize that the papers are for all different types of things that I have to do, so I decide instead to sort them into groups of similar tasks, in which case I'll have several "to do" piles that will be more manageable than one large stack of papers.

This is when it dawns on me that I will have to read all the sheets of paper so I can know what is written on them, and that will help me determine what needs to be done with each one, like if I need to write a summary for one thing, create a spread sheet for another, write a reference letter for someone, or calculate some other types of data. Then, I can put all the sheets of paper in my desk drawer once the work is done.

I pull open the large drawer on the side of my desk, which is the drawer that has the hanging file folders, and I see that each one is labeled, and that should certainly be helpful, I think optimistically. If I can get the tasks done from each sheet, I figure, I can put those sheets of paper in the correct files. Without reading them, however, I won't know what to do, and the thought of reading them is so overwhelming at this moment that I instead decide to divide the sheets into separate piles of ten sheets each, counting carefully and pulling apart the ones that are stapled together. That way I can tackle one set of ten papers a day, I decide.

So now, with careful counting and stacking, my desk is covered with eleven sets of paper, ten sheets each. I stand back to look at the stacks, and they look pretty well organized to me. Time to start reading, I think to myself, but then it occurs to me that maybe some tasks will be pretty big ones and others smaller, so maybe ten things a day will be too much, especially given that I don't know what the tasks are since I haven't read the papers. Maybe I should just read one sheet a day, I decide.

Therefore, since I need to lay them out one at a time, I gather the piles into one stack and take it into the living room, since it is larger than my cramped dining room, and I begin to place each sheet carefully, one at a time, in a row across the living room floor, all facing up, ready to go. I start on one side of the room and begin putting the sheets across the length of the room until I get to the end, and then I start another row, and so on, until the floor is completely covered with sheets of paper. Now I can just grab one sheet and read it and see what I need to do.

I stand back to look at my living room floor, and I am suddenly completely overwhelmed. It is definitely too much work. I walk out of the room, take a deep breath, and close the hall doorway so I won't have to see my work again. Maybe I can wait until dark, I think, when I can sneak in the room and grab one sheet off the floor before feeling overwhelmed, and I can jump right into the first task before giving it too much thought.

Although some of the sheets of paper likely have pressing matters that I probably need to attend to, I also begin to consider the idea that most of them can probably just be ignored, even thrown right into the trash and nobody at work will notice. I decide that I will contemplate this more pleasant idea a bit more tomorrow because now I am very tired, so I walk back into the dining room and stand there, admiring my newly-organized desk, the top of which is now completely cleaned off.

The sudden loud ringing of my house phone interrupts my wandering thoughts, and I stand there holding my ears while it rings and rings and rings like it is never going to end, drilling into my ears to give me an earache, and finally the ringing switches over to the answering machine.

I continue to stand there, while listening to my own voice impart a cheery message and explain that I am not available but I will return your call as soon as humanly possible! So very soon!! Once my recorded message ends, the answering machine switches over to the voice of my colleague, who is now leaving me a message.

"How are you doing?" she begins, hesitantly. "We are getting a bit worried about you, not just because the report is due and you promised to work on it from home, but also because we are just wondering how you are doing, so please call back when you get this message," she continues, and then hangs up.

"Very sad," I think to myself, "sad that this is happening. I really need to figure this shit out!" This time I can't tell if I said that to myself in my mind or out loud.

Just then, a sharp pain shoots through my head, signaling the beginning of a migraine. I have been having a lot of these lately. The sunlight is raking across the room now, pulsing and moving on the floor, making my head hurt even worse. Even though my hands are shaking and my legs feel weak, I decide that the next thing I need to do is to push my desk away from the wall and move it next to the dining room table because I want to make a blanket fort, like when Jack was little. The desk is heavy, but I manage to scrape it across the floor, leaving two rows of scratched wood along the way. I then retrieve two blankets and one large comforter from the hall closet and return to the dining room to drape the blankets so they stretch across the table and down the side of the desk.

In my desk drawer are several rolls of leftover spaceship silver duct tape, so I put thick strips of the tape along the edges of both blankets to secure them to the table legs, but the tape doesn't stick to the fabric very well so I wrap the tape across the table and down the other side, then under the table and back up the opposite side until the roll is empty. I take the comforter and cover the floor and put the small desk lamp under the table, making sure the extension cord reaches across from the outlet. I pat down the comforter but the floor still seems hard beneath it, so I get a sleeping bag and two pillows from my bedroom closet and put them on the comforter to make a cozy, soft area under the table that stretches out beneath the desk. I kneel down on the floor and crawl under the table to see that the fort is just the same as what I remembered making when Jack was a little boy. We used to hide under the blankets for hours, reading books by the lamplight.

Suddenly my headache stabs me with a vengeance, so now I wish I had thought to get a few aspirins when I was in my bedroom finding the pillows and before crawling under the desk because it will take a pretty big effort to get back out and go down to my bedroom a second time. I lie there and try to figure out if the headache is bad enough to merit that kind of effort, and I decide that since the kitchen is closer, I can get my bottle of wine instead because that will stop my headache and put me to sleep, even better. Then, once I wake up I can get right to work typing up things and getting tasks completed. I am really thinking ahead now!

I crawl out from under my desk, stand up very slowly so I don't get dizzy, and I walk carefully toward the kitchen. It is never good to fall down when you are home alone, just like in that TV commercial where the woman is lying there at the base of her stairway screaming, "I have fallen and can't get up!" I don't want that to happen to me because who would take care of Jack? By now my leg is shaking so much that I have to move even more slowly toward the pantry, like I am swimming underwater.

I remember that before Christmas I hid several wine bottles behind the potato bin in the pantry to keep them away from Jack. I hide so many things these days—money, keys, alcohol, medicine bottles, lighters and matches, my telephone, that I am less and less able to remember where everything is, but I find not two but three wine bottles in the pantry, bingo. Fortunately they have twist-off caps since I have not been able to find the corkscrew that I hid from Jack a while back, so I take two of the bottles under the table with me and open one of them. The cap slips out of my hand and buries itself in the folds of the sleeping bag, so I hold the bottle in one hand, trying really hard to remember to keep the bottle upright so it doesn't spill, while I dig around the sleeping bag with my other hand. This is my fort, and I don't want wine spilled all over it.

When Jack was little, sometimes he couldn't sleep. We would drag our blankets into the dining room and throw them over the table and get our pillows and sheets to spread on the floor beneath the table. Then we would sit inside the fort, hidden from the world, and read stories until I grew so tired that my head would start to nod, and each time I would begin to fall asleep, Jack would poke my arm with his chubby finger, trying to keep me awake so I could read to him a bit longer.

He always wanted me to keep reading on and on, and although I was always so tired, I really did try. However, in my half-waking half-sleeping state, the words would slide down and spill off the page, and although I would strain my eyes to try to read them straight across one after another, the lines would dissolve in front of my eyes.

In that way, the stories I told Jack would drift away from their original plot toward a new narrative, one that blended the written word with my dream world where the story would become a word salad spoken straight from my subconscious. Jack knew each book by heart, he could recite all their words from memory even before he learned to read them. Therefore he knew when the story strayed, and he would get impatient with me as I drifted from the waking world to the sleeping world, and sometimes, when he poked me awake with his fingers, I would hear the echo of my own words hanging in the air, words that wove an entirely different tale from the one we began reading.

"Tell me the right story!" he would demand.

Jack would then laugh bitterly at me and accuse me of changing the endings and not making sense on purpose, so I would jerk my eyes back open and try really hard to finish the story as it was written. I wanted to stay awake for Jack and I didn't want to disappoint him, but in the end I was never able to stay awake, and so every night the last thing I would see as I drifted off to sleep was Jack's chubby round face positioned right in front of mine with his blue eyes staring at me impatiently, waiting to hear the end of a story. But it was always too late; I was already in the dreaming.

———————

I wake up a few hours later to see the shadows lengthening in my dining room, making the room darker and cooler. I smell alcohol and realize that I am lying in the wet sticky wine that has tipped over and soaked into the sleeping bag. I now remember that I am under my dining room table, so I peer out from beneath the blanket to assess the situation, while my headache starts back again as my eyes scan the floor of the room. The rest of the house seems silent, so I start to crawl out from under the table on my hands and knees, cautiously, slowly, in order not to startle myself, and when I see the empty room, I am relieved. I look at the clock on the wall in the kitchen and it says 7:15 p.m., I think, unless the time is wrong, which is a possibility, so I stumble into the living room, where the clock says 3:09 a.m.

Now I am not sure what to do, but I start to think about why it matters what time it is, especially since I don't even remember what day it is. In fact, I am hoping it is the later time so I can just go to bed. If I can stay like this in my house, living smoothly, gliding along as if I am swimming underwater with everything tamped down and slow like molasses, maybe I can get things figured out, I think to myself. I walk into the kitchen to get a drink of water and swallow a few more pills for this headache that seems to be spreading into my shoulders and neck.

After I swallow four pills, I look down at the bottle and see that they are the blue pills, the oval ones. I am thinking that aspirin is a round white pill, chalky tasting, but these taste like plastic. I wish I hadn't transferred Jack's pills into different bottles because now I can't remember the name of the blue pills, but since I only took four of them, I figured I would be OK.

I put the bottle back down and saunter crookedly back into the living room as if I am dragging my feet through sand. I glance down at the floor just to make sure it isn't covered in sand. I mean…I know it really isn't, but it doesn't hurt to check, right? I bend down to touch the floor, making sure there isn't anything else there that is making my feet so heavy. Guess not. I stand in the middle of the room now. If I just take a little break, I think, I can definitely figure out my next move, the next thing I need to do.

Just then I hear the sound of footsteps on the front porch and I panic and lurch around in a small circle, not sure where to go, so I try to run back to the desk, but I slip and fall on the floor in my sock feet. I fall with a dull thud that doesn't hurt at all, so very strange. I have a clear view into the hallway where I watch myself fall in the hall mirror and observe my arms flying upward like they are made of string, while my body lifts up off the ground. I don't have time to recover from my fall, however, because next I hear the screen door creaking open and the heavy knob of the front door start to twist and rattle. That door is always so hard to open, I think as I get up on my hands and knees and crawl the rest of the way back to the table where I dive beneath the blankets just as the front door swings open.

I am under the table trying to calm my breath so nobody can hear me when Jack calls out to me quizzically, "Mom?" like he is asking a question. I contemplate not answering because I don't want him to see me like this, so I lie very still under the desk. I hear his feet move toward me, and then I hear nothing. He must be stopping in front of the desk like in a horror movie, so I try to remain very still even though I am shaking all over.

"Mom?" he asks again. I see his feet now, wearing his white Vans without the laces that are positioned in front of my face on the other side of the blanket. I decide that I should answer.

"Yes?" I say, as if I am asking a question. I try to make my voice sound natural but the single word comes out loud and squeaky. Now I am crying, so I quickly wipe my tears off my cheeks just as I see Jack's face peeking in at me, then he is staring at me with the blanket lifted up and framing his face. At first he looks at me impatiently, then with a puzzled expression, and he smiles a little bit in a way that I haven't seen in a long time. It isn't a big smile, but it is something.

The blanket flaps down over his face as he drops his whole body to the floor and he lifts the blanket again, but this time he crawls on his hands and knees under the blanket and sits next to me, hunched down beneath the table. When he was a boy he could sit under the table crisscross applesauce, but now he can barely fit his long body sideways the length of the table.

"What the hell are you doing under here?" he asks.

I try to answer but I gasp out something unintelligible, words now seem to elude me. Instead, I suddenly feel sick to my stomach and focus my attention on trying to fight back my nausea.

"I am just trying to figure all this shit out," I finally respond.

"Nothing to figure out," Jack says, staring at me with an attention span I haven't seen in a long time.

I draw in a sharp breath, gasping for air. Now it is very hot under the blanket, like a sauna, which makes it difficult to breathe so I try to suck more air into my lungs in big gulps, but it doesn't seem to help. I lean over to the corner of the fort and vomit onto the floor, and then I cover up the vomit with an edge of the sleeping bag. Maybe this little medical experiment was a big mistake, I think to myself.

Jack is still staring at me but I can't figure out what he is thinking. We are both sitting on the other end of the sleeping bag that is still slightly damp from the spilled wine, and we are resting our elbows on the two pillows next to us.

"Mom, I've been thinking a lot about the

journey I'm taking, since I am the Fool." I look up at Jack's face, trying to focus on a point between his eyes.

"I've been thinking about it for a long time and I know you're worried I'm going to step off the precipice," he continues.

A tear rolls down my cheek when I hear him say this.

"The view from above is so amazing, though, Mom, I wish you could see it. From here I can see the entire world," he explains with a sense of urgency, willing me to know what he is saying.

I nod my head up and down; I want to understand. "But I've been thinking," he continues, "that after I see everything, I could just as easily turn around and walk back down the mountain and re-join the world and share what I've seen."

Now I do understand. I continue nodding my head maybe a little too vigorously until gray spots float across my field of vision.

"That sounds good, really good," I gurgle. I need to lie down, so I grab both pillows and rest my head on them while Jack watches me intently. The last thing I remember is his face tilted down toward mine, with his blue eyes burning through me, asking, "Mom, do you want me to read you a story?"

Acknowledgements

Many people in the medical profession have been very helpful to me and to my son. I thank the staff at the Central Oklahoma Community Mental Health Center in Norman, Oklahoma, which was one of the first community centers built in the United States and is a model for excellent healthcare. The Children's Recovery Center, Red Rock Behavioral Health Services, Norman Regional Hospital and Griffin Memorial Hospital in Norman, Oklahoma; the Oklahoma Crisis Intervention Center and Cedar Ridge Hospital in Oklahoma City; Shepherd Hill Behavioral Health in Newark, Ohio, and Twin Valley Behavioral Healthcare in Columbus, Ohio, all helped my son over the years. The faculty and staff at Norman High School and Denison University were very kind during my son's time as a student at both places.

In particular, I want to thank the psychiatrist who answered my son's pharmacological questions in detail without talking down to him; the nurse who returned my phone calls promptly despite her busy schedule; the counselor who looked me in the eye and asked me how I was doing; the staff member who gave my son a big farewell hug; the security guard who talked with my son about his dreams; and the workers at Second Chance Animal Sanctuary who let my son walk their rescue dogs. Finally, I am thankful for my son's friends who stayed around not just for the manic fun but also for the crappy dark stuff. This book would not exist without my son Julian, who inspired parts of this story.

Made in the USA
Columbia, SC
14 December 2017